MacClintock

SONG AND LEGEND FROM THE MIDDLE AGES

UUID: e8ce7f76-1fb6-11e9-a5a5-17532927e555

This ebook was created with StreetLib Write

http://write.streetlib.com

Table of contents

PREFACE. 1
INTRODUCTION. 3
I. THE NATIONAL EPIC. 7
II. ROMANCES. 8
III. LYRICS. 10
IV. TALES AND FABLES. 11
V. DIDACTIC AND ALLEGORICAL LITERATURE. 12
VI. THE DRAMA. 13
SONG AND LEGEND FROM THE MIDDLE AGES. 14
CHAPTER I. FRENCH LITERATURE. 15
CHAPTER II. SPANISH LITERATURE. 76
CHAPTER III. SCANDINAVIAN LITERATURE. 99
CHAPTER IV. GERMAN LITERATURE. 114
CHAPTER V. ITALIAN LITERATURE. 174

PREFACE.

The aim of this little book is to give general readers some idea of the subject and spirit of European Continental literature in the later and culminating period of the Middle Ages—the eleventh, twelfth, and thirteenth centuries.

It goes without saying that translations and selections are, in general, inadequate to the satisfactory representation of any literature. No piece of writing, of course, especially no piece of poetry, can be perfectly rendered into another tongue; no piece of writing can be fairly represented by detached portions. But to the general English reader Continental Mediaeval literature, so long as it remains in the original tongues, is inaccessible; and translations of many entire works are not within easy reach.

What translation and selection can do in this case, is to put into the hands of the ordinary student of the Middle Ages sufficient material for forming an estimate of the subjects that interested the mediaeval mind and the spirit in which they were treated. And this is what the general reader desires. Matters of form and expression—the points that translation cannot reproduce—belong, of course, to the specialist.

The claim that so slender a volume of selections can represent even the subject and spirit of so vast a body of literature, is saved from being unreasonable or presumptuous by a consideration of the fact that, from causes easy to trace, the national literatures of Continental Europe had many common characteristics: the range of subjects was not unlimited; the spirit is the same in all.

No English is included for two reasons: Mediaeval English literature is easily accessible to those readers for whom this book is prepared; during the special period in which the best mediaeval literature was developed, England was comparatively unproductive.

The constant aim has been to put before the reader the literature itself, with comment barely sufficient to make an intelligible setting for the selections. Criticism of all kinds has been avoided, so that the reader may come to his material with judgment entirely unbiased. The translations used have been selected largely with a view to their accessibility, so that readers who desire to enlarge the scope of their reading may easily find the books they need. Caxton's "Reynard the Fox", and "The Romance of the Rose", attributed to Chaucer, were chosen because they convey an impression of the quaint flavor of the original, which is lost in a modern version. The slight adaptations and transliterations made in these two selections are entirely defensible on the score of intelligibility.

Our acknowledgments are due to Prof. William I. Knapp, of the University of Chicago, for the use of books from his valuable library, and for the permission, most highly prized, to print for the first time some of his translations of the Cid ballads.

THE EDITORS. Chicago, April, 1893.

INTRODUCTION.

The Middle Ages extend from the fifth to the fifteenth century, from the fall of the Roman Empire to the establishment of the great modern states. The general outline of the history of the Middle Ages can be seen in the following excellent table:[1]

[1] Drury's "History of the Middle Ages", page XIV.

1. The decline of the Roman Empire and the successful accomplishment of two invasions.

2. The transient brilliancy of the Arabian civilization.

3. The attempted organization of a new empire by Charlemagne, and its dissolution.

4. The rise and prevalence of feudalism.

5. The successive crusades.

6. The contest between the pope and the emperor for the sovereignty of the world.

The history of these ten centuries falls naturally into three great divisions:

1. Fifth to tenth century, the destruction of the past and transition to new forms.

2. Eleventh to thirteenth century, feudal society with its customs, its institutions, its arts, and its literatures.

3. The fourteenth and fifteenth centuries, a second time of transition.

The period, then, of the eleventh, twelfth, and thirteenth centuries was one of intense political life, of advanced national self-consciousness, of rich, highly-organized society. It was moreover a period of common ideas, movements, and tendencies over all Europe. Several factors enter into this result:

1. The church was completely organized, forming a common life and teaching everywhere. She had learned to employ the savage vigor and conquering instincts of the northern barbarians as defenses and aggressive missions of her spirit and ideas. The monasteries were homes of learning, and from them issued the didactic literature and the early drama.

2. This resulted in that romantic institution or ideal of chivalry, whose ten commandments explain so much of mediaeval life and art.[1]

[1] "Chivalry", by Leon Gautier, 1891, p. 26.

(1) Thou shalt believe all the church teaches, and shalt observe all its directions.

(2) Thou shalt defend the church.

(3) Thou shalt respect all weaknesses, and shalt constitute thyself the defender of them.

(4) Thou shalt love the country in which thou wast born.

(5) Thou shalt not recoil before thine enemy.

(6) Thou shalt make war against the inflael without cessation and without mercy.

(7) Thou shalt perform scrupulously thy feudal duties, if they be not contrary to the law of God.

(8) Thou shalt never lie, and shalt remain faithful to thy pledged word.

(9) Thou shalt be generous and give largesse to every one.

(10) Thou shalt be everywhere and always the champion of the Right and the Good against Injustice and Evil.

3. This combination of the Christian and the warrior found its public activity most completely in the Crusades. They gave a common motive and ideal to all the knights of Europe. They brought them together for thinking and for fighting. They spread national traditions and literatures. They made the whole face of Europe and the borders of the Mediterranean known to the ambitious, venturesome, daring, and heroic of every European country. The exploits of chivalric knights were told from camp to camp and taken back home to be told again in the castles.

4. Another institution of feudalism that helped to make this common subject and spirit of mediaeval literature was the minstrel, who was attached to every well-appointed castle. This picturesque poet—gleeman, trouvere or troubadour sang heroic stories and romances of love in the halls of castles and in the market places of towns. He borrowed from and copied others and helped to make the

common method and traditions of mediaeval song.

5. Other elements in this result were the extensions of commerce and the growth of traveling as a pleasure.

6. Finally, the itinerant students and teachers of mediaeval universities assisted in the making of this common fund of ideas and material for literature.

(7) Behind and within all the separate national literatures lay the common Christian-Latin literature of the early Middle Ages, undoubtedly the cause of the rather startling perfection of form shown by much of the work of the period we are studying.[1]

[1] See Ebert "Allgemeine Geschichte der Literatur des Mittelalters". Vol. I., p. 11.

The result of all these unifying tendencies is to give a strong family likeness to the productions of the various European countries of the eleventh, twelfth, and thirteenth centuries. The subject matter often varies, but the motive and form of writing are much alike. This likeness can be seen by a short survey of the more important kinds of literature of the period.

I. THE NATIONAL EPIC.

In every country in which the national epic grew up it had the same origin and line of development. First there was the historical hero. His deeds were related by the traveling gleeman or minstrel—in brief chapters or ballads. Gradually mythical and supernatural elements came in; the number of achievements and the number of ballads grew very large; in this oral state they continued for many years, sometimes for centuries.

Finally, they were collected, edited, and written down—generally by a single editor. In all cases the names of the poets of the ballads are lost; in most cases the names of their redactors are but conjectural. "The Song of Roland", and the "Poem of the Cid" are typical, simple, national epics. The "Niebelungen Lied" is complicated by the fact that the legends of many heroes are fused into one poem, by the fact that it had more than one editor, and by the survival of mythological elements which mingle confusedly with Christian features. The national epic is the expression of the active side of chivalry. Italy has no national epic, both because she was too learned to develop a folk-poetry, and because the ideas of chivalry were never very active in her history.

II. ROMANCES.

The numberless romances that sprang up in the literary period of the Middle Ages may be thrown into three groups:

1. Those belonging to the legend of Arthur and the Round Table. They had their starting point in the history of Geoffrey of Monmouth, which was partly invented, but had some basis in a tradition common to the Bretons and the Welsh. The romances based upon this legend sprang up apparently simultaneously in England and France. Through minstrel romances, founded upon the Breton popular tradition, the Arthur legend probably first found its way into European literature. With it was early fused the stories of the Holy Grail and of Parzival. In the twelfth century these stories were widely popular in literary form in France and Germany, and later they passed into Italy, Spain, and Scandinavia. Their influence upon the life and thought of Mediaeval Europe is very important. They did much to modify the entire institution of chivalry.[1]

[1] Leon Gautier's "Chivalry", chap. IV., Section V.

2. The Romances of Antiquity, of which there are three varieties:

(1) Those which were believed to be direct reproduc-

tions, such as the Romances of Thebes, of Aeneas, of Troy, whose authors acknowledged a debt to Vergil, Statius, and other classic writers.

(2) Those based upon ancient history not previously versified, such as the Romance of Alexander.

(3) Those which reproduced the names and nothing else from antiquity.

These romances, too, were a common European possession. The most important and influential of them are the Romance of Troy, and the Romance of Alexander. They appear in different forms in the literature of every mediaeval nation in Europe.

3. There was in each national literature a vast number of unaffiliated romances. A romance of this group usually contained a love story, a tale of adventure, or a religious experience in the form of a story. They are not clearly distinct from the class of popular tales. On the whole, the romance is more serious and dignified than the tale. Examples of this kind of a romance are Hartmann von Aue's "Henry the Leper", and the French "Flore et Blanchefleur".

III. LYRICS.

Perhaps no other part of its literature shows more striking proof of the common life and interests of Mediaeval Europe than does the lyric poetry of the period. In Northern France, in Provence, in all parts of Germany, in Italy, and a little later in Spain, we see a most remarkable outburst of song. The subjects were the same in all the countries. Love-the love of feudal chivalry—patriotism, and religion were the themes that employed the mediaeval lyrist in whatever country he sang. In all these lyrics much was made of form, the verse being always skillfully constructed, sometimes very complicated. The lyric poetry of Italy was more learned and more finished in style than that of the other countries.

In Northern France the poet was called a trouvere, in Provence a troubadour, in Germany a minnesinger. The traveling minstrel was in France a jongleur (Provencal jogleur). The distinction between trouvere or troubadour and jongleur is not always to be sharply drawn. Sometimes in France and Provence the same poet composed his verses and sang them—was both trouvere or troubadour and jongleur; while in Germany the minnesingers were generally both poets and minstrels.

IV. TALES AND FABLES.

No distinct line can be drawn between Tales and Fables; between Romances and Tales; nor between Fables and Allegories. These varieties of writings merge into one another.

The number of tales in circulation in Mediaeval Europe was exceedingly large. These tales came from many different sources: from Oriental lands, introduced by the Moors, or brought back by the crusaders; from ancient classical literature; from traditions of the church and the lives of the saints; from the old mythologies; from common life and experience. Among many mediaeval collections of them, the most famous are the "Decameron" of Boccaccio, and the "Geste Romanorum", a collection made and used by the priests in instructing their people.

V. DIDACTIC AND ALLEGORICAL LITERATURE.

Under didactic literature we would include a large mass of writing not strictly to be called pure literature—sermons, homilies, chronicles, bestiaries, and chronologies. Nearly all these were written in verse, as prose did not begin to be used for literature until very late in the Middle Ages. The mediaeval mind, under the influence of the scholastic theology, grew very fond of allegory. The list of allegories is exhaustless, and some of the allegories well-nigh interminable. It is not easy to say whether the "Romance of Reynard the Fox" is a series of fables or an allegory. The fact that a satire on human affairs runs through it constantly, warrants us in calling it an allegory. Some phase of the Reynard legend formed the medium of expression of the thought of every mediaeval nation in Europe. Perhaps the most popular and influential allegory of the Middle Ages was "The Romance of the Rose", written in France but translated or imitated in every other country. Dante's "Divine Comedy" is an allegory of a very elevated kind.

VI. THE DRAMA.

The origin and line of development of the drama in all the countries of Mediaeval Europe is this: Dramatic representations in connection with the liturgy of the church were first used in the service; then they were extended to church festivals and ceremonies. By degrees portions of Bible history were thrown into dramatic form; then the lives of the saints furnished material. A distinction grew up between Mystery Plays—those founded on Bible history—and Miracle Plays—those founded on the lives of the saints. These plays were performed both in the churches and in the open air. They were written usually by the clergy. Gradually there grew up a play in which the places of religious characters were taken by abstract virtues and vices personified, and plays called Moralities were produced. They were played chiefly by tradesmen's guilds. Alongside the sacred drama are to be found occasional secular dramatic attempts, farces, carnival plays, and profane mysteries. But their number and significance are small. The mediaeval drama is historically interesting, but in itself does not contain much interest. It is impossible to give an idea of it by selection.

SONG AND LEGEND FROM THE MIDDLE AGES.

CHAPTER I. FRENCH LITERATURE.

French Literature of the Middle Ages was produced between the eleventh and the fifteenth centuries, having its greatest development in the twelfth and thirteenth centuries. It must be divided into two sections according to the part of France where it was produced.

I. French Literature proper, or that composed in the northern half of France.

II. Provencal Literature, or that developed in Provence.

The most obvious difference between these is that the Provencal literature had little of the epic and romantic, but developed the lyric extensively, especially lyrics of love.

The following table will show the more important kinds of French
Mediaeval Literature.[1]

[1] This classification is adapted from M. Gaston Paris' excellent sketch "La Litterature Francaise au Moyen Age", 1890, and Saintsbury's "Short History of French Literature",

1889.

    I. Narrative Literature.

    1. The National Epics.

    2. Romances of Antiquity.

    3. Arthurian Romances.

    4. Romances of Adventure.

    5. Tales and Fables.

    6. Chronicles.

    II. Didactic Literature.

    1. Allegories—"The Romance of the Rose".

    2. Satires.

    3. Homilies, etc.

    III. Lyric Literature.

THE NATIONAL EPICS.

The French national epics (called "Chansons de Gestes", songs of heroic deeds) are those narrative poems which are founded on early French history, and recount the deeds of national heroes. They are, for the most part, based on the deeds of Charlemagne and his nobles. They are peculiar to Northern France. Their date of production extends from the eleventh to the fourteenth century, their best development being in the eleventh and twelfth.

These epic poems number more than one hundred. They vary in length from one thousand to thirty thousand lines. The whole mass is said to contain between two and three million lines. Like all folk epics, they are based upon earlier ballads composed by many different poets. These ballads were never written down and are completely lost. The epic is a compilation and adaptation, presumably by a single poet, of the material of the ballads. In every case the names of the poets of the French epics are lost. They were trouveres and their poems were carried about in memory or in manuscript by the jongleurs or minstrels, and sung from castle to castle and in the market places. The best of them are: "The Song of Roland"; "Amis et Amiles"; "Aliscans"; "Gerard de Roussillon"; "Raoul de Cambrai". Of these the oldest and confessedly the greatest is The Song of Roland, from which our extracts are taken.

The Song of Roland is based upon the following events (the events as narrated in the poem differ widely from those of the actual history): Charlemagne has warred seven years in Spain, when Marsile, king of Saragossa, the only city that has withstood the emperor, sends a feigned submission. Roland, the king's nephew, offers to go to Saragossa to settle the terms of the treaty. He is rejected as too impetuous, when he suggests that Ganelon go. This bitterly annoys Ganelon, and when he meets Marsile he makes a treacherous plot by which Charlemagne is to be induced to go back to France, with Roland in command of the rear guard. The plan works, and when the advanced party of the French army is out of reach, the Saracens fall upon the rear guard in the pass of Roncevalles and completely destroy it. The death of Roland, the return and grief of the king, and his vengeance on the pagans form the central incident of the poem. Ganelon is afterwards tried for his treachery, condemned, and executed.

THE SONG OF ROLAND.

Stanza I.—
The king, our Emperor Carlemaine,
Hath been for seven full years in Spain.
From highland to sea hath he won the land;
City was none might his arm withstand;
Keep and castle alike went down—
Save Saragossa, the mountain town.
The King Marsilius holds the place,
Who loveth not God, nor seeks His grace:
He prays to Apollin, and serves Mahound;
But he saved him not from the fate he found.

King Marsile held a council and decided to offer Charlemagne a feigned submission. Karl summons his council to consider this.

Stanza 8.—
King Karl is jocund and gay of mood,
He hath Cordres city at last subdued;
Its shattered walls and turrets fell
By catapult and mangonel;
Not a heathen did there remain
But confessed himself Christian or else was slain.
The Emperor sits in an orchard wide,
Roland and Olivier by his side:
Samson the duke, and Anseis proud;
Geoffrey of Anjou, whose arm was vowed
The royal gonfalon to rear;
Gereln, and his fellow in arms, Gerier:
With them many a gallant lance,

Full fifteen thousand of gentle France.
The cavaliers sit upon carpets white
Playing at tables for their delight;
The older and sager sit at chess,
The bachelors fence with a light address.
Seated underneath a pine,
Close beside an eglantine,
Upon a throne of beaten gold,
The lord of ample France behold;
White his hair and beard were seen,
Fair of body, and proud of mien,
Who sought him needed not ask, I ween.
The ten alight before his feet,
And him in all observance greet.

The treacherous plot has succeeded. Charles, with the main part of his army, has gone ahead, the Saracens have fallen on the rear-guard, and are destroying it. Oliver begs Roland to sound his wonderful horn and summon aid.

Stanza 87.—
"O Roland, sound on your ivory horn,
To the ear of Karl shall the blast be borne:
He will bid his legions backward bend,
And all his barons their aid will lend."
"Now God forbid it, for very shame,
That for my kindred were stained with blame,
Or that gentle France to such vileness fell:
This good sword that hath served me well,
My Durindana such strokes shall deal,
That with blood encrimsoned shall be the steel.

By their evil star are the felons led;
They shall all be numbered among the dead!"

    Stanza 88.—
"Roland, Roland, yet wind one blast!
Karl will hear ere the gorge be passed,
And the Franks return on their path fall fast!
"I will not sound on mine ivory horn:
It shall never be spoken of me in scorn,
That for heathen felons one blast I blew;
I may not dishonour my lineage true.
But I will strike, ere this fight be o'er,
A thousand strokes and seven hundred more,
And my Durindana will drip with gore.
Our Franks shall bear them like vassals brave.
The Saracens shall flock but to find a grave."

    Stanza 89.—
"I deem of neither reproach nor stain.
I have seen the Saracen host of Spain,
Over plain and valley and mountain spread,
And the regions hidden beneath their tread.
Countless the swarm of the foe, and we
A marvellous little company."
Roland answered him, "All the more
My spirit within me burns therefore.
God and the angels of heaven defend
That France through me from her glory bend.
Death were better than fame laid low.

Our Emperor loveth a downright blow."

At last Roland blows his horn, but it is too late. All the Moors are slain or routed, but so are all the Franks save Roland, and he has received his death blow.

Stanza 195—
That Death was on him he knew full well;
Down from his head to his heart it fell.
On the grass beneath a pinetree's shade,
With face to earth his form he laid,
Beneath him placed he his horn and sword,
And turned his face to the heathen horde.
Thus hath he done the sooth to show,
That Karl and his warriors all may know,
That the gentle count a conqueror died.
Mea Culpa full oft he cried;
And, for all his sins, unto God above,
In sign of penance, he raised his glove.

Stanza 197.—
Beneath a pine was his resting-place,
To the land of Spain hath he turned his face.
On his memory rose full many a thought
Of the lands he won and the fields he fought;
Of his gentle France, of his kin and line;
Of his nursing father King Karl benign;
He may not the tear and sob control,
Nor yet forgets he his parting soul.
To God's compassion he makes his cry:

"O Father true, who canst not lie,
Who didst Lazarus raise unto life again,
And Daniel shield in the lions' den;
Shield my soul from its peril, due
For the sins I sinned my lifetime through."
He did his right hand glove upliftst.
Gabriel took from his hand the gift;
Then drooped his head upon his breast,
And with clasped hands he went to rest.
God from on high sent down to him
One of his angel cherubim—
Saint Michael of Peril of the sea,
Saint Gabriel in company—
From heaven they came for that soul of price,
And they bore it with them to Paradise.

The king hears Roland's horn and hurries back, only to find him and all his knights slain. He swoons, revives, but swoons again.

Stanza 212.—
As Karl the king revived once more,
His hands were held by barons four.
He saw his nephew, cold and wan;
Stark his frame, but his hue was gone;
His eyes turned inward, dark and dim;
And Karl in love lamented him:
"Dear Roland, God thy spirit rest
In paradise, amongst His blest!
In evil hour thou soughtest Spain:
No day shall dawn but sees my pain,

And me of strength and pride bereft,
No champion of mine honour left;
Without a friend beneath the sky;
And though my kindred still be nigh,
Is none like thee their ranks among."
With both his hands his beard he wrung.
The Franks bewailed in unison;
A hundred thousand wept like one.

    Stanza 213.—
"Dear Roland, I return again
To Laon, to mine own domain;
Where men will come from many a land,
And seek Count Roland at my hand.
A bitter tale must I unfold—
'In Spanish earth he lieth cold.'
A joyless realm henceforth I hold,
And weep with daily tears untold.

    Stanza 214—
"Dear Roland, beautiful and brave,
All men of me will tidings crave,
When I return to La Chapelle.
Oh, what a tale is mine to tell!
That low my glorious nephew lies.
Now will the Saxon foeman rise;
Palermitan and Afric bands,
And men from fierce and distant lands.
To sorrow sorrow must succeed;

My hosts to battle who shall lead,
When the mighty captain is overthrown?
Ah! France deserted now, and lone.
Come, death, before such grief I bear."
Began he with his hands to tear;
A hundred thousand fainted there.

    Stanza 215.—
"Dear Roland, and was this thy fate?
May Paradise thy soul await.
Who slew thee wrought fair France's bane:
I cannot live so deep my pain.
For me my kindred lie undone;
And would to Holy Mary's Son,
Ere I at Cizra's gorge alight,
My soul may take its parting flight:
My spirit would with theirs abide;
My body rest their dust beside."
With sobs his hoary beard he tore.
"Alas!" said Naimes, "for the Emperor."

    The Franks take terrible vengeance on the Moors who survive. Then they bury their dead comrades and all return to France.

    Stanza 225.
—From Spain the Emperor made retreat,
To Aix in France, his kingly seat;
And thither, to his halls, there came,
Alda, the fair and gentle dame.

"Where is my Roland, sire," she cried,
"Who vowed to take me for his bride?
O'er Karl the flood of sorrow swept;
He tore his beard and loud he wept.
"Dear Sister, gentle friend," he said,
"Thou seekest one who lieth dead:
I plight to thee my son instead,—
Louis, who lord of my realm shall be."
"Strange," she said, "this seems to me.
God and his angels forbid that I
Should live on earth if Poland die."
Pale grow her cheek—she sank amain,
Down at the feet of Carlemaine.
So died she. God receive her soul!
The Franks bewail her in grief and dole.

    Stanza 226.—
So to her death went Alda fair.
The king but deemed she fainted there.
While dropped his tears of pity warm,
He took her hands and raised her form.
Upon his shoulder drooped her head,
And Karl was ware that she was dead.
When thus he saw that life was o'er,
He summoned noble ladies four.
Within a cloister was she borne;
They watched beside her until morn;
Beneath a shrine her limbs were laid;
Such honour Karl to Alda paid.

ROMANCES.

Another form of narrative literature in the Middle Ages is that of Romances, and the great products of it are the Arthurian Romances and the Romances of Antiquity. THE ARTHURIAN CYCLE OF ROMANCES is a set of romantic stories founded on the legends of Arthur and the Knights of the Round Table, with which was early fused the legend of the Holy Graal. The legend has sources as far back as the ninth century, but expanded into definite shape in France and England in the twelfth. It had its first and highest popular development in France. Here they were collected and thrown into verse by Chrestien de Troyes. It became at once a general European possession and expanded to vast proportions. In England the Arthur stories flourished both independently and as translations from French. Sir Thomas Malory collected in the latter part of the fifteenth century a great number of these sources, translated, edited, abridged, and rewrote the whole into that charming book "Morte D'Arthur". It is accepted that this book, though so late, gives a true impression of the characteristics of the older romances. We select from this rather than from other translations of French originals, to give a mediaeval flavor to the selection and have the advantage of quoting a classic.

Alongside the Arthurian Romances, flourished many romances of antiquity. The more important of these cycles are the ROMANCE OF ALEXANDER and the ROMANCE OF TROY, while others worth mentioning are the ROMANCE OF THEBES and the ROMANCE OF AENEAS. They are all very long poems, consisting of series of stories partly derived from classic sources, partly invented by trouveres. They are important (1) as connecting, however loosely, mediaeval with classical literature, and (2) as showing some scholarship on the part of their authors and interest in general culture.

FROM MORTE D'ARTHUR.
Book I. Chapter 23.

How Arthur by the mean of Merlin gat Excalibur his sword of the
Lady of the lake.

Right so the king and he departed, and went until an hermit that was a good man and a great leach. So the hermit searched all his wounds and gave him good salves; so the king was there three days, and then were his wounds well amended that he might ride and go, and so departed. And as they rode, Arthur said, I have no sword. No force, said Merlin, hereby is a sword that shall be yours and I may. So they rode till they came to a lake, the which was a fair water and broad, and in the midst of the lake Arthur was ware of an arm clothed in white samite, that held a fair sword in that hand. Lo, said Merlin, yonder is that sword that I spake of. With that they saw a damsel going upon the lake: What damsel is that? said Arthur. That is the Lady of the lake, said Merlin; and within that lake is a rock, and therein is as fair a place as any on earth, and richly beseen, and this damsel will come to you anon, and then speak ye fair to her that she will give you that sword. Anon withal came the damsel unto Arthur and saluted him, and he her again. Damsel, said Arthur, what sword is that, that yonder the arm holdeth above the water? I would it were mine' for I have no sword. Sir Arthur king, said the damsel, that sword is mine, and if ye will give me a gift when I ask it you, ye shall have it. By my faith, said Arthur, I will give you what gift ye will ask. Well, said the damsel, go ye into yonder barge and row yourself to the sword, and take it and the scabbard with you, and I will ask my gift when I see my time. So Sir Arthur and Merlin alight, and tied their horses to two trees, and so they went into the ship, and when they came to the sword that the hand held, Sir Arthur took it up by the handles, and took it with him. And the arm and the hand went under the water; and so they came unto the land and rode forth.

Book III. Chapter 1.

How king Arthur took a wife, and wedded Guenever daughter to
Leodegrance, king of the land of Cameliard, with whom he had the
Round Table.

In the beginning of Arthur, after he was chosen king by adventure and by grace—for the most part of the barons knew not that he was Uther Pendragon's son, but as Merlin made it openly known,—many kings and lords made great war against him for that cause; but well Arthur overcame them all; for the most part of the days of his life he was ruled much by the council of Merlin. So it fell on a time king Arthur said unto Merlin, My barons will let me have no rest, but needs I must take a wife, and I will none take but by thy council and by thine advice. It is well done, said Merlin, that ye take a wife, for a man of your bounty and nobleness should not be without a wife. Now is there any that ye love more than another? Yea, said king Arthur, I love Guenever, the daughter of king Leodegrance, of the land of Cameliard, which Leodegrance holdeth in his house the Table Round, that ye told he had of my father, Uther. And this damsel is the most valiant and fairest lady that I know living, or yet that ever I could find. Sir, said Merlin, as of her beauty and fairness she is one of the fairest on live. But and ye loved her not so well as ye do, I could find you a damsel of beauty and of goodness that should like you and please you, and your heart were not set; but there as a man's heart is set, he will be loth to return. That is truth, said king Arthur. But Merlin warned the king covertly that Guenever was not wholesome for him to take to wife, for he warned him that Launcelot should love her, and she him again; and so he turned his tale to the adventures of the Sangreal. Then Merlin desired of the king to have men with him that should enquire of Guenever, and so the king granted him. And Merlin went forth to king Leodegrance of Cameliard, and told him of the desire of the king that he would have unto his wife Guenever his daughter. That is to me, said king Leodegrance, the best tidings that ever I heard, that so worthy a king of prowess and noblesse will wed my daughter. And as for my lands I will give him wist I it might please him, but he hath lands enough, him needeth none, but I shall send him a gift shall please him much more, for I shall give him the Table Round, the which Uther Pendragon gave me, and when it is full complete there is an hundred knights and fifty. And as for an hundred good knights I have myself, but I lack fifty, for so many have been slain in my days. And so king Leodegrance delivered his daughter Guenever unto Merlin, and the Table Round, with the hundred knights, and so they rode freshly, with great royalty, what by water and what by land, till that they came nigh unto London.

Book III. Chapter 2.

How the knights of the Round Table were ordained, and their sieges blessed by the bishop of Canterbury.

When king Arthur heard Of the coming of Guenever and the hundred knights with the Table Round, then king Arthur made great joy for their coming, and that rich present, and said openly, This fair lady is passing welcome unto me, for I have loved her long, and therefore there is nothing so lief to me. And these knights with the Round Table please me more than right great riches. And in all haste the king let ordain for the marriage and the coronation in the most honourablest wise that could be devised. Now Merlin, said king Arthur, go thou and espy me in all this land fifty knights which be of most prowess and worship. Within short time Merlin had found such knights that should fulfil twenty and eight knights, but no more he could find. Then the bishop of Canterbury was fetched, and he blessed the sieges with great royalty and devotion, and there set the eight and twenty knights in their sieges. And when this was done Merlin said, Fair sirs, ye must all arise and come to king Arthur for to do him homage; he will have the better will to maintain you. And so they arose and did their homage. And when they were gone Merlin found in every siege letters of gold that told the knights' names that had sitten therein. But two sieges were void: And so anon came young Gawaine, and asked the king a gift. Ask, said the king, and I shall grant it you. Sir, I ask that ye will make me knight that same day ye shall wed fair Guenever. I will do it with a good will, said king Arthur, and do unto you all the worship that I may, for I must by reason you are my nephew, my sister's son.

It is now the Vigil of the feast of Pentecost, and the knights are all at Arthur's court. Sir Launcelot is suddenly desired to go on a mission by a fair damsel who takes him to a forest and an abbey.

Book XIII. Chapter 1.

Truly, said Sir Launcelot, a gentlewoman brought me hither, but I know not the cause. In the meanwhile, as they thus stood talking together, there came twelve nuns which brought with them Galahad, the which was passing fair and well made, that unneth in the world men might not find his match; and all those ladies wept. Sir, said the ladies, we bring you here this child, the which we have nourished, and we pray you to make him a knight; for of a more worthier man's hand may he not receive the order of knighthood. Sir Launcelot beheld that young squire, and saw him seemly and demure as a dove, with all manner of good features, that he wend of his age never to have seen so fair a man of form. Then said Sir Launcelot, Cometh this desire of himself? He and all they said, Yea. Then shall he, said Sir Launcelot, receive the high order of knighthood as tomorrow at the reverence of the high feast. That night Sir Launcelot had passing good cheer, and on the morn at the hour of prime, at Galahad's desire, he made him knight, and said, God make him a good man, For beauty faileth you not as any that liveth.

Sir Launcelot returns to court. It is noticed that the back of the "siege (seat) perilous," at the Round Table has a new inscription saying that this day this long unfilled seat should be filled. Before sitting down to feast on this day, it was an old custom to see "some adventure."

Book XIII. Chapter 2.

So as they stood speaking, in came a squire, and said unto the king, Sir, I bring unto you marvellous tidings. What be they? said the king. Sir, there is here beneath at the river a great stone, which I saw fleet above the water, and therein saw I sticking a sword. The king said, I will see that marvel. So all the knights went with him, and when they came unto the river, they found there a stone fleeting, as it were of red marble, and therein stack a fair and a rich sword, and in the pomell thereof were precious stones, wrought with subtil letters of gold. Then the barons read the letters, which said in this wise: Never shall man take me hence but only he by whose side I ought to hang, and he shall be the best knight of the world. When the king had seen these letters, he said unto Sir Launcelot, Fair sir, this sword ought to be yours, for I am sure ye be the best knight of the world. Then Sir Launcelot answered full soberly: Certes, sir, it is not my sword: also, sir, wit ye well I have no hardiness to set my hand to, for it longed not to hang by my side. Also who that assayeth to take that sword, and falleth of it, he shall receive a wound by that sword, that he shall not be whole long after. And I will that ye wit that this same day will the adventures of the Sancgreal, that is called the holy vessel, begin.

Sir Gawaine tries to draw out the sword but fails. They sit at table and an old man brings in the young knight, Sir Galahad.

Book XIII. Chapter 4.

Then the old man made the young man to unarm him;

and he was in a coat of red sendel, and bare a mantle upon his shoulder that was furred with ermine, and put that upon him. And the old knight said unto the young knight, Sir, follow me. And anon he led him unto the siege perilous, where beside sat Sir Launcelot, and the good man lift up the cloth, and found there letters that said thus: This is the siege of Galahad the haut prince. Sir, said the old knight, wit ye well that place is yours. And then he set him down surely in that siege . . . . Then all the knights of the Table Round marvelled them greatly of Sir Galahad, that he durst sit there in that siege perilous, and was so tender of age, and wist not from whence he came, but all only by God, and said, This is he by whom the Sancgreal shall be achieved, for there sat never none but he, but he were mischieved.

King Arthur showed the stone with the sword in it to Sir Galahad. He lightly drew out the sword and put it in his sheath. Then the king had all his knights come together to joust ere they departed.

Book XIII. Chapter 6.
Now, said the king, I am sure at this quest of the Sancgreal shall all ye of the Table Round depart, and never shall I see you again whole together, therefore I will see you all whole together in the meadow of Camelot, to just and to tourney, that after your death men may speak of it, that such good knights were wholly together such a day. As unto that council, and at the king's request, they accorded ill, and took on their harness that longed unto justing. But all this moving of the king was for this intent, for to see Galahad proved, for the king deemed he should not lightly come again unto the court after his departing. So were they

assembled in the meadow, both more and less. Then Sir Galahad, by the prayer of the king and the queen, did upon him a noble jesserance, and also he did on his helm, but shield would he take none for no prayer of the king. And then Sir Gawaine and other knights prayed him to take a spear. Right so he did; and the queen was in a tower with all her ladies for to behold that tournament. Then Sir Galahad dressed him in the midst of the meadow, and began to break spears marvellously, that all men had wonder of him, for he there surmounted all other knights, for within a while he had thrown down many good knights of the Table Round save twain, that was Sir Launcelot and Sir Percivale.

Book XIII. Chapter 7.

And then the king and all estates went home unto Camelot, and so went to evensong to the great minster. And so after upon that to supper, and every knight sat in his own place as they were toforehand. Then anon they heard cracking and crying of thunder, that them thought the place should all to- drive. In the midst of this blast entered a sun-beam more clearer by seven times than ever they saw day, and all they were alighted of the grace of the Holy Ghost. Then began every knight to behold other, and either saw other by their seeming fairer than ever they saw afore. Not for then there was no knight might speak one word a great while, and so they looked every man on other, as they had been dumb. Then there entered into the hall the holy Graile covered with white samite, but there was none might see it, nor who bare it. And there was all the hall full filled with good odours, and every knight had such meats and drinks as he best loved in this world: and when the holy Graile had been borne through the hall, then the holy vessel departed suddenly, that they wist not where it became. Then had they all breath to speak. And then the king yielded thankings unto God of his good grace that he had sent them. Certes, said the king, we ought to thank our Lord Jesu greatly, for that he hath shewed us this day at the reverence of this high feast of Pentecost. Now, said Sir Gawaine, we have been served this day of what meats and drinks we thought on, but one thing beguiled us, we might not see the holy Graile, it was so preciously covered: wherefore I will make here avow, that to-morn, without longer abiding, I shall labour in the quest of the Sancgreal, that I shall hold me out a twelvemonth and a day, or more if need be, and never shall I return again unto the court till I have seen it more openly than it hath been seen here; and if I may not speed, I shall return again as he that may not be against the will of our Lord Jesu Christ. When they of the Table Round heard Sir Gawaine say so, they arose up the most party, and made such avows as Sir Gawaine had made.

Book XVII. Chapter 20.

How Galahad and his fellows were fed of the holy Sangreal, and how our Lord appeared to them, and other things. Then king Pelles and his son departed. And therewithal beseemed them that there came a man and four angels from heaven, clothed in likeness of a bishop, and had a cross in his hand, and these four angels bare him up in a chair, and set him down before the table of silver whereupon the Sancgreal was, and it seemed that he had in midst of his forehead letters that said, See ye here Joseph the first bishop of Christendom, the same which our Lord succoured in the city of Sarras, in the spiritual place. Then the knights marvelled, for that bishop was dead more than three hundred years tofore. Oh knights, said he, marvel not, for I was sometime an earthly man. With that they heard the chamber door open, and there they saw angels, and two bare candles of wax, and the third a towel, and the fourth a spear which bled marvellously, that three drops fell within a box which he held with his other hand. And they set the candles upon the table, and the third the towel upon the vessel, and the fourth, the holy spear even upright upon the vessel. And then the bishop made semblant as though he would have gone to the sacring of the mass. And then he took an ubbly, which was made in likeness of bread; and at the lifting up there came a figure in likeness of a child, and the visage was as red and as bright as any fire, and smote himself into the bread, so that they all saw it, that the bread was formed of a fleshly man, and then he put it into the holy vessel again. And then he did that longed to a priest to do to a mass. And then he went to Galahad and kissed him, and bad him go and kiss his fellows, and so he did anon. Now, said he, servants of Jesu Christ, ye shall be fed afore this table with sweet meats, that never knights tasted. And when he had said, he vanished away; and they set them at the table in great dread, and made their prayers. Then looked they, and saw a man come out of the holy vessel, that had all the signs of the passion of Jesu Christ, bleeding all openly, and said, My knights and my servants and my true children, which be come out of deadly life into spiritual life, I will now no longer hide me from you, but ye shall see now a part of my secrets and of my hid things: now hold and receive the high meat which ye have so much desired. Then took he himself the holy vessel, and came to Galahad, and he kneeled down and there he received his Saviour, and after him so received all his fellows; and they thought it so sweet that it was marvellous to tell. Then said he to Galahad, Son, wotest thou what I hold betwixt my hands? Nay, said he, but if ye will tell me. This is, said he, the holy dish wherein I ate the lamb on Sher-thursday. And now hast thou seen that thou most desiredst to see, but yet hast thou not seen it so openly as thou shalt see it in the city of Sarras, in the spiritual place.

LYRIC POETRY—FRENCH.

Lyric poetry sprang up very early in Northern France, having a spontaneous and abundant growth in the twelfth and thirteenth centuries. Of the earliest lyrics, the critics distinguish two varieties (l) the Romance, and (2) the Pastourelle. These are generally dramatic love stories, full of gay and simple life and extremely artistic and musical in form. Along with these was produced a vast amount of simple lyric poetry on love and other personal emotions. The number of poems written was immense. About two hundred names of poets have come down to us, besides hundreds of anonymous pieces.

The Romances and Pastourelles of the northern trouveres were soon greatly influenced by the more artful poetry of the Provencal troubadours, producing the highly artificial but charming rondeaus and ballades of the fourteenth and fifteenth centuries. But the freshest, most individual work is that of the earlier time.

CHATELAIN DE COUCY. Thirteenth Century.

The first approach of the sweet spring

Returning here once more,—
The memory of the love that holds
In my fond heart such power,—
The thrush again his song assaying,—
The little rills o'er pebbles playing,
And sparkling as they fall,—
The memory recall
Of her on whom my heart's desire
Is, shall be, fixed till I expire.

   With every season fresh and new
That love is more inspiring:
Her eyes, her face, all bright with joy,—
Her coming, her retiring,
Her faithful words, her winning ways,—
That sweet look, kindling up the blaze,
Of love, so gently still,
To wound, but not to kill,—
So that when most I weep and sigh,
So much the higher springs my joy.

   — Tr. by Taylor.

THIBAUT OF CHAMPAGNE, KING OF NAVARRE.
Early Thirteenth Century.
   Lady, the fates command, and I must go,—
Leaving the pleasant land so dear to me:
Here my heart suffered many a heavy woe;
But what is left to love, thus leaving thee?
Alas! that cruel land beyond the sea!

Why thus dividing many a faithful heart,
Never again from pain and sorrow free,
Never again to meet, when thus they part?

    I see not, when thy presence bright I leave,
How wealth, or joy, or peace can be my lot;
Ne'er yet my spirit found such cause to grieve
As now in leaving thee; and if thy thought
Of me in absence should be sorrow-fraught,
Oft will my heart repentant turn to thee,
Dwelling in fruitless wishes, on this spot,
And all the gracious words here said to me.

    O gracious God! to thee I bend my knee,
For thy sake yielding all I love and prize;
And O, how mighty must that influence be,
That steals me thus from all my cherished joys!
Here, ready, then, myself surrendering,
Prepared to serve thee, I submit; and ne'er
To one so faithful could I service bring,
So kind a master, so beloved and dear.

    And strong my ties,—my grief unspeakable!
Grief, all my choicest treasures to resign;
Yet stronger still the affections that impel
My heart toward Him, the God whose love is mine.
That holy love, how beautiful! how strong!
Even wisdom's favorite sons take refuge there;

'T is the redeeming gem that shines among
Men's darkest thoughts,—for ever bright and fair.

— Tr. by Taylor.

GACE BRULE. Thirteenth Century.
　The birds, the birds of mine own land
I heard in Brittany;
And as they sung, they seemed to me
The very same I heard with thee.
And if it were indeed a dream,
Such thoughts they taught my soul to frame
That straight a plaintive number came,
Which still shall be my song,
Till that reward is mine which love hath promised long.

— Tr. by Taylor.

RAOUL DE SOISSONS. Thirteenth Century.
　Ah! beauteous maid,
Of form so fair!
Pearl of the world,
Beloved and dear!
How does my spirit eager pine
But once to press those lips of thine!—
Yes, beauteous maid,
Of form so fair!
Pearl of the world,
Beloved and dear!

And if the theft
Thine ire awake,
A hundred fold
I'd give it back,—
Thou beauteous maid,
Of form so fair!
Pearl of the world,
Beloved and dear!

— Tr. by Taylor.

LATER FRENCH LYRICS.

During the latter half of the thirteenth century several new and highly artificial forms of verse were developed. The chief of these were the Ballade and Chant Royal, the Rondel, Roudeau, Triolet, Virelay. These are all alike in being short poems, generally treating of love, and making special use of a refrain and the repetition of words and lines. They differ in the number of verses in a stanza, of stanzas In the poem, and the order and number of rhymes. Their poetic value is not great because the poet so easily lost sight of his subject in perfecting his verse form.

A TRIOLET.

Take time while yet it is in view,
For fortune is a fickle fair:
Days fade, and others spring anew;
Then take the moment still in view.
What boots to toil and cares pursue?
Each month a new moon hangs in air.

Take, then, the moment still in view,
For fortune is a fickle fair.

— Froissart. Tr. Anonymous.

RONDEL.

Now Time throws off his cloak again
Of ermined frost, and cold and rain,
And clothes him in the embroidery
Of glittering sun and clear blue sky.
With beast and bird the forest rings,
Each in his jargon cries or sings;
And Time throws off his cloak again
Of ermined frost, and cold and rain.

River, and fount, and tinkling brook
Wear in their dainty livery
Drops of silver jewelry;
In new-made suit they merry look;
And Time throws off his cloak again
Of ermined frost, and cold and rain.

— Charles d'Orleans. Tr. by Longfellow.

THE BALLADE OF DEAD LADIES.

Tell me now in what hidden way is
Lady Flora the lovely Roman?
Where's Hipparchia, and where is Thais,
Neither of them the fairer woman?

Where is Echo, beheld of no man,
Only heard on river and mere,—
She whose beauty was more than human? ....
But where are the snows of yester-year?

Where's Heloise, the learned nun,
For whose sake Abeillard, I ween,
Lost manhood and put priesthood on?
(From love he won such dule and teen!)
And where, I pray you, is the Queen
Who willed that Buridan should steer
Sewed in a sack's mouth down the Seine? ....
But where are the snows of yester-year?

White Queen Blanche, like a queen of lilies,
With a voice like any mermaiden,—
Bertha Broadfoot, Beatrice, Alice,
And Ermengarde the lady of Maine,—
And that good Joan whom Englishmen
At Rouen doomed and burned her there,—
Mother of God, where are they then? ....
But where are the snows of yester-year?

Nay, never ask this week, fair lord,
Where they are gone, nor yet this year,
Save with thus much for an overword,—
But where are the snows of yester-year?

— Villon. Tr. by D. G. Rossetti.

LYRIC POETRY—PROVENCAL.

Modern scholars separate the treatment of Provencal literature from that of French. It was written in a different dialect, was subject to somewhat different laws of development, and after a short period of activity died almost completely away.

Provencal literature is that produced in ancient Provence or Southern France. Its period of life extended from the eleventh to the fifteenth centuries, its middle and only important period being that of the twelfth and thirteenth centuries. This literature contains examples of all the varieties of French literature of the Middle Ages, but the only work that is original and important is its lyric poetry. This was composed by the troubadours (corresponding to the French trouveres) and sung by jongleurs or minstrels. The names of 460 Provencal poets and 251 anonymous pieces have come down to us. The one great theme of troubadour-singing—one, too, upon which he was original and a master—was that of passionate love. With this as subject, these poets united an eagerness for form, and were the first to perfect verse in any modern language.

PIERRE ROGIERS. Twelfth Century.
Who has not looked upon her brow
Has never dreamed of perfect bliss,
But once to see her is to know
What beauty, what perfection, is.

Her charms are of the growth of heaven,
She decks the night with hues of day:
Blest are the eyes to which 't is given
On her to gaze the soul away!

— Tr. by Costello.

GUILLEM DE CABESTANH. Twelfth Century.

No, never since the fatal time
When the world fell for woman's crime,
Has Heaven in tender mercy sent—
All preordaining, all foreseeing—
A breath of purity that lent
Existence to so fair a being!
Whatever earth can boast of rare,
Of precious, and of good,—
Gaze on her form, 't is mingled there,
With added grace endued.

Why, why is she so much above
All others whom I might behold,
Whom I, unblamed, might dare to love,
To whom my sorrows might be told?
O, when I see her, passing fair,
I feel how vain is all my care:
I feel she all transcends my praise,
I feel she must contemn my lays:
I feel, alas! no claim have I
To gain that bright divinity!
Were she less lovely, less divine,
Less passion and despair were mine.

— Tr. by Costello.

THE MONK OF MONTAUDON. Thirteenth Century.

I love the court by wit and worth adorned,
A man whose errors are abjured and mourned,
My gentle mistress by a streamlet clear,
Pleasure, a handsome present, and good cheer.

I love fat salmon, richly dressed, at noon;
I love a faithful friend both late and soon.

I hate small gifts, a man that's poor and proud,
The young who talk incessantly and loud;
I hate in low-bred company to be,
I hate a knight that has not courtesy.
I hate a lord with arms to war unknown,
I hate a priest or monk with beard o'ergrown;
A doting husband, or a tradesman's son,
Who apes a noble, and would pass for one.
I hate much water and too little wine,
A prosperous villain and a false divine;
A niggard lout who sets the dice aside;
A flirting girl all frippery and pride;
A cloth too narrow, and a board too wide;
Him who exalts his handmaid to his wife,
And her who makes her groom her lord for life;
The man who kills his horse with wanton speed,
And him who fails his friend in time of need.

— Tr. by Costello.

PIERRE VIDAL. End Twelfth Century.
Of all sweet birds, I love the most
The lark and nightingale:
For they the first of all awake,
The opening spring with songs to hail.

And I, like them, when silently
Each Troubadour sleeps on,
Will wake me up, and sing of love
And thee, Vierna, fairest one!
. . . .
The rose on thee its bloom bestowed,
The lily gave its white,
And nature, when it planned thy form
A model framed of fair and bright.

For nothing, sure, that could be given,
To thee hath been denied;
That there each thought of love and joy
In bright perfection might reside.

— Tr. by Taylor.

GUIRAUT DE BORNEILH. End Thirteenth Century.
Companion dear! or sleeping or awaking,
Sleep not again! for, lo! the morn is nigh,
And in the east that early star is breaking,
The day's forerunner, known unto mine eye.

The morn, the morn is near.

    Companion dear! with carols sweet I'll call thee;
Sleep not again! I hear the birds' blithe song
Loud in the woodlands; evil may befall thee,
And jealous eyes awaken, tarrying long,
Now that the morn is near.

    Companion dear! forth from the window looking,
Attentive mark the signs of yonder heaven;
Judge if aright I read what they betoken:
Thine all the loss, if vain the warning given.
The morn, the morn is near.

    Companion dear! since thou from hence wert straying,
Nor sleep nor rest these eyes have visited;
My prayers unceasing to the Virgin paying,
That thou in peace thy backward way might tread.
The morn, the morn, is near.

    Companion dear! hence to the fields with me!
Me thou forbad'st to slumber through the night,
And I have watched that livelong night for thee;
But thou in song or me hast no delight,
And now the morn is near.

ANSWER.

Companion dear! so happily sojourning,
So blest am I, I care not forth to speed:
Here brightest beauty reigns, her smiles adorning
Her dwelling-place,—then wherefore should I heed
The morn or jealous eyes?

— Tr. by Taylor.

FABLES AND TALES.
FABLES.

A large and popular class of writing of the French Middle Ages was that of FABLIAUX or Fables. A Fable is "a recital, for the most part comic, of a real or possible event occurring in the ordinary affairs of human life."[1] We possess some two hundred of these fables, varying in length from twenty to five hundred lines. They are generally mocking, jocular, freespoken, half satirical stories of familiar people, and incidents in ordinary life. The follies of the clergy are especially exposed, though the peasants, knights, and even kings furnish frequent subjects. They are commonly very free and often licentious in language. The following is an example of the simpler kind of Fables.

[1] Quoted by Saintsbury from M. de Montaiglon, editor of the latest collection of Fabliaux (Parts 1872-'88).

THE PRIEST WHO ATE MULBERRIES.
Ye lordlings all, come lend an ear;

It boots ye naught to chafe or fleer,
As overgrown with pride:
Ye needs must hear Dan Guerin tell
What once a certain priest befell,
To market bent to ride.

    The morn began to shine so bright,
When up this priest did leap full light
And called his folk around:
He bade them straight bring out his mare,
For he would presently repair
Unto the market-ground.

    So bent he was on timely speed,
So pressing seemed his worldly need,
He weened 't were little wrong
If pater-nosters he delayed,
And cast for once they should be said
E'en as he rode along.

    And now with tower and turret near
Behold the city's walls appear,
When, as he turned aside,
He chanced in evil hour to see
All hard at hand a mulberry-tree
That spread both far and wide.

Its berries shone so glossy black,
The priest his lips began to smack,
Full fain to pluck the fruit;
But, woe the while! the trunk was tall,
And many a brier and thorn did crawl
Around that mulberry's root.

The man, howbe, might not forbear,
But reckless all he pricked his mare
In thickest of the brake;
Then climbed his saddle-bow amain,
And tiptoe 'gan to stretch and strain
Some nether bough to take.
A nether bough he raught at last;
He with his right hand held it fast,
And with his left him fed:
His sturdy mare abode the shock,
And bore, as steadfast as a rock,
The struggling overhead.

So feasted long the merry priest,
Nor much bethought him of his beast
Till hunger's rage was ended:
Then, "Sooth!" quoth he, "whoe'er should cry,
'What ho, fair sir!' in passing by,
Would leave me here suspended."

Alack! for dread of being hanged,

With voice so piercing shrill he twanged
The word of luckless sound,
His beast sprang forward at the cry,
And plumb the priest dropped down from high
Into the brake profound.

    There, pricked and pierced with many a thorn,
And girt with brier, and all forlorn,
Naught boots him to complain:
Well may ye ween how ill bested
He rolled him on that restless bed,
But rolled and roared in vain:

    For there algates he must abide
The glowing noon, the eventide,
The livelong night and all;
The whiles with saddle swinging round,
And bridle trailing on the ground,
His mare bespoke his fall.

    O, then his household shrieked for dread,
And weened at least he must be dead;
His lady leman swooned:
Eftsoons they hie them all to look
If haply in some dell or nook
His body might be found.

Through all the day they sped their quest;
The night fled on, they took no rest;
Returns the morning hour:
When, lo! at peeping of the dawn.
It chanced a varlet boy was drawn
Nigh to the mulberry-bower.

The woful priest the help descried:
"O, save my life! my life!" he cried,
"Enthralled in den profound!
O, pluck me out, for pity's sake,
From this inextricable brake,
Begirt with brambles round!"

"Alas, my lord! my master dear!
What ugly chance hath dropped thee here?"
Exclaimed the varlet youth.
"'T was gluttony'" the priest replied,
With peerless folly by her side:
But help me straight, for ruth!"

By this were come the remnant rout;
With passing toil they plucked him out,
And slowly homeward led:
But, all so tattered in his hide,
Long is he fain in bed to bide,
But little less than dead.

— Tr. by Way.

A special development of the fable is the mock-epic "Reynard the Fox", one of the most noteworthy developments in literature of the Middle Ages. It is an elaborate, semi-epic set of stories in which Reynard is the embodiment of cunning and discreet valor, while his great enemy, Isegrim, the wolf, represents stupid strength. From the beginning of this set of fables, there is a tone of satirical comment on men and their affairs. In the later developments of the story, elaborate allegories are introduced, and monotonous moralizings take the place of the earlier, simpler humor.

The fable reached its greatest development in France, but all
Europe shared in making and delighting in it.

Our extracts are taken from Caxton's translation of the Flemish form of the legend.

FROM REYNARD THE FOX.

Part II. Chapter 33.

REYNARD AND ERSWYNDE (THE WOLF'S WIFE) AT THE WELL.

Then spoke Erswynde, the wolf's wife, "Ach! Fell Reynard, no man can keep himself from thee, thou canst so well utter thy words and thy falseness; but it shall be evil, rewarded in the end. How broughtest thou me once, into the well, where the two buckets hung by one cord running through one pulley which went one up and another down? Thou sattest in one bucket beneath in the pit in great dread. I came thither and heard thee sigh and make sorrow, and asked thee how thou camest there. Thou saidst that thou hadst there so many good fishes eaten out of the water that thy belly wouldst burst. I said, 'tell me how I shall come to thee.' Then saidst thou: 'Aunt, spring into that bucket that hangeth there, and thou shalt come anon to me.' I did so, and I went downward and ye came upward, and then I was all angry. Thou saidst, 'thus fareth the world, that one goeth up and another goeth down.' Then sprang ye forth and went your way, and I abode there alone, sitting an whole day, sore and hungry and acold. And thereto had I many a stroke ere I could get thence." "Aunt," said the fox, "though the strokes did you harm, I had leifer ye had them than I, for ye may better bear them, for one of us must needs have had them. I taught you good; will you understand it and think on it, that ye another time take heed and believe no man over hastily, is he friend or cousin. For every man seeketh his own profit. They be now fools that do not so, and especially when they be in jeopardy of their lives."

Part II. Chapter 35.

HOW ISEGRYM PROFFERED HIS GLOVE TO THE FOX FOR TO FIGHT WITH HIM.

The wolf said, "I may well forbear your mocks and your scorns, and also your fell, venomous words' strong thief that you are. Ye said that I was almost dead for hunger when ye helped me in my need. That is falsely lied; for it was but a bone that ye gave to me; ye had eaten away all the flesh that was thereon. And ye mock me and say that I am hungry here where I stand. That touched my worship too nigh. What many a spighty word have ye brought forth with false lesings.[1] And that I have conspired the king's death, for the treasure that you have said to him is in Hulsterlo. And ye have also my wife shamed and slandered that she shall never recover it. And I should ever be disworshipped thereby if I avenged it not. I have forborne you long, but now ye shall not escape me. I cannot make here of great proof, but I say here before my lord, and before all them that been here, that thou art a false traitor and a murderer, and that I shall prove and make good on thy body within lists in the field, and that, body against body. And then shall our strife have an end. And thereto I cast to thee my glove, and take thou it up. I shall have right of thee or die therefor.

[1] Lyings.

Reynard the Fox thought, "how came I on this company? We been not both alike.[1] I shall not well con[2] stand against this strong thief. All my proof is now come to an end."

[1] Of equal strength. [2] Know how to.

Yet, thought the fox, "I have good advantage. The claws of his fore feet been off and his feet been yet sore thereof, when for my sake he was unshod. He shall be somewhat the weaker."

Then said the fox, "who that sayeth that I am a traitor or a murderer? I say he lieth falsely, and that art thou especially Isegrym. Thou bringest me there as I would be. This have I oft desired. Lo! there is my pledge that all thy words been false and that I shall defend me and make good that thou liest.

The king received the pledges and amitted[1] the battle, and asked borrows[2] of them both, that on the morn they should come and perform their battle and do as they ought to do. Then the Bear and the Cat were borrows for the wolf, and for the Fox were borrows Grymbert,[3] the dasse,[4] and Bytelnys.[5]

[1] Admitted. [2] Pledges. [3] The badger. [4] A small fox. [5] The elder daughter of the apes.

TALES.

French mediaeval literature includes many tales less elaborate in form and less "heroic" in subject than the epics and romances and without the satire and humor of the fables. The best of them are the love stories, and of these the most beautiful is "Aucassin and Nicolette", by an unknown trouvere of the thirteenth century. It is an alternation of prose narrative and dainty narrative lyrics. The story is that of two lovers parted temporarily by the pride and cruelty of the youth's father. But, remaining true to each other, they are, after many vicissitudes, happily united. Our extracts are from Bourdillon's beautiful translation.

FROM AUCASSIN AND NICOLETTE.

Sec. 1.—
Who were fain good verse to hear,
Of the aged captives' cheer,
Of two children fair and feat,
Aucassin and Nicolette,—
What great sorrows suffered he,
And what deeds did valiantly
For his love, so bright of blee?

Sweet the song, and fair the say,
Dainty and of deft array.
So astonied wight is none,
Nor so doleful nor undone,
None that doth so sorely ail,
If he hear, shall not be hale,
And made glad again for bliss,
So sweet it is!

The hero refuses to become a knight and go to war unless his father will give him Nicolette for wife.

Sec. 8.—
Aucassin was of Beaucaire,
And abode in castle fair.
None can move him to forget
Dainty-fashioned Nicolette
Whom his sire to him denies;
And his mother sternly cries:
"Out on thee! what wilt thou, loon?
Nicolette is blithe and boon?
Castaway from Carthage she!
Bought of Paynim compayne!
If with woman thou wilt mate,
Take thee wife of high estate!"
"Mother, I can else do ne'er!
Nicolette is debonair;
Her lithe form, her face, her bloom,
Do the heart of me illume.
Fairly mine her love may be
So sweet is she!"

This the father refuses to do, and has Nicolette shut up in a tower. But the son stubbornly persists. At last it is agreed that if Aucassin returns from fighting he may see and kiss his lover.

Sec. 9.—
Aucassin heard of the kiss
Which on return shall be his.
Had one given him of pure gold
Marks a hundred thousand told,
Not so blithe of hear he were.
Rich array he bade them bear:
They made ready for his wear.
He put on a hauberk lined,
Helmet on his head did bind,
Girt his sword with hilt pure gold,
Mounted on his charger bold;
Spear and buckler then he took;
At his two feet cast a look:
They trod in the stirrups trim.
Wondrous proud he carried him
His dear love he thought upon,
And his good horse spurred anon,
Who right eagerly went on.
Through the gate he rode straightway,
Into the fray.

Aucassin was greatly successful, but on his return his father would not keep his promise, and shut him up in prison.

Sec. 12.— Aucassin was put in prison, as you have listened and heard, and Nicolette on the other hand, was in the chamber. It was in the summer-time, in the month of May, when the days are warm, long, and bright, and the nights still and cloudless. Nicolette lay one night on her bed and saw the moon shine bright through a window, and heard the nightingale sing in the garden, and then she bethought her of Aucassin, her friend, whom she loved so much. She began to consider of the Count Garin of Beaucaire, who hated her to death; and she thought to herself that she would remain there no longer; since if she were betrayed, and the Count Garin knew it, he would make her to die an evil death. She perceived that the old woman who was with her was asleep. She got up, and put on a gown which she had, of cloth-of-silk and very good; and she took bedclothes and towels, and tied one to another, and made a rope as long as she could, and tied it to the pillar of the window, and let herself down into the garden; and she took her dress in one hand before and in the other behind, and tucked it up, because of the dew which she saw thick on the grass, and she went away down in the garden.

Her hair was golden and in little curls, and her eyes blue-gray and laughing, and- her face oval, and her nose high and well set, and her lips vermeil, so as is no rose nor cherry in summertime, and her teeth white and small, and her bosom was firm, and heaved her dress as if it had been two walnuts; and atween the sides she was so slender that you could have clasped her in your two hands; and the daisy blossoms which she broke off with the toes of her feet, which lay fallen over on the bend of her foot, were right black against her feet and her legs, so very white was the maiden.

She came to the postern door, and unfastened it, and went out through the streets of Beaucaire, keeping in the shadow, for the moon shone very bright; and she went on till she came to the tower where her lover was. The tower was shored up here and there, and she crouched down by one of the pillars, and wrapped herself in her mantle; and she thrust her head into a chink in the tower, which was old and ruinous, and heard Aucassin within weeping and making great ado, and lamenting for his sweet friend whom he loved so much. And when she had listened enough to him she began to speak.

After telling each their love, Nicolette was obliged to flee. She went to a great forest and talked with the herd-boys.

Sec. 19.—
Nicolette, bright-favored maid,
To the herds her farewell bade,
And her journey straight addressed
Right amid the green forest,
Down a path of olden day;
Till she reached an open way
Where seven roads fork, that go out
Through the region round about.
Then the thought within her grew,
She will try her lover true,
If he love her as he said:
She took many a lily head,
With the bushy kermes-oak shoot,
And of leafy boughs to boot,

And a bower so fair made she,—
Daintier I did never see!
By the ruth of heaven she sware,
Should Aucassin come by there,
And not rest a little space,
For her love's sake' in that place,
He should ne'er her lover be,
Nor his love she.

Aucassin escapes, comes to the forest, finds his lover, and they agree to go away together.

Sec. 27—
Aucassin, the fair, the blond,
Gentle knight and lover fond,
Rode from out the thick forest;
In his arms his love was pressed,
On the saddlebow before;
And he kissed her o'er and o'er,
Eyes and brows and lips and chin.
Then to him did she begin;

"Aucassin, fair lover sweet,
To what country shall we fleet?
"Sweet my love, what should I know?
Little care I where we go,
In the greenwood or away,
So I am with thee alway."
Hill and vale they fleeted by,
Town and fortress fenced high,

Till they came at dawn of day
Where the sea before them lay;
There they lighted on the sand,
Beside the strand.

They have many adventures and are again separated. Nicolette is carried to Carthage. She finally escapes and makes her way in disguise to Beaucaire where Aucassin was.

Sec. 39.—
Aucassin was at Beaucaire
'Neath the tower a morning fair.
On a stair he sat without,
With his brave lords round about:
Saw the leaves and flowers spring,
Heard the song-birds carolling;
Of his love he thought anew,
Nicolette the maiden true,
Whom he loved so long a day;
Then his tears and sighs had way.
When, behold before the stair,
Nicolette herself stood there,
Lifted viol, lifted bow,
Then she told her story so:
"Listen, lordlings brave, to me,
Ye that low or lofty be!
Liketh you to hear a stave,
All of Aucassin the brave,
And of Nicolette the true?
Long they loved and long did rue,

Till into the deep forest
After her he went in quest.
From the tower of Torelore
Them one day the Paynim bore,
And of him I know no more.
But true-hearted Nicolette
Is in Carthage castle yet;
To her sire so dear is she,
Who is king of that countrie.
Fain they would to her award
Felon king to be her lord.
Nicolette will no Paynim,
For she loves a lording slim,
Aucassin the name of him.
By the holy name she vows
That no lord will she espouse,
Save she have her love once moe
She longs for so!"

She is at last revealed to him, and all ends happily.

Sec. 41.—
Now when Aucassin did hear
Of his own bright favored fere,
That she had arrived his shore,
Glad he was as ne'er before.
Forth with that fair dame he made
Nor until the hostel stayed.
Quickly to the room they win,
Where sat Nicolette within.
When she saw her love once more,

Glad she was as ne'er before.
Up she sprang upon her feet,
And went forward him to meet.
Soon as Aucassin beheld,
Both his arms to her he held,
Gently took her to his breast,
All her face and eyes caressed.
Long they lingered side by side;
And the next day by noontide Aucassin her lord became;
Of Beaucaire he made her Dame.
After lived they many days,
And in pleasure went their ways.
Now has Aucassin his bliss,
Likewise Nicolette ywis.
Ends our song and story so;
No more I know.

DIDACTIC LITERATURE.

France produced, along with its heroic poetry, its romances, tales, and lyrics, much serious and allegorical work. This was in the shape of homilies, didactic poems, and long allegories touching manners and morals. Of these last the most famous and important is "The Romance of the Rose". It was the most popular book of the Middle Ages in France. It was begun by William of Lorris about 1240, the first draft extending to 4670 lines. Some forty years later, Jean de Meung, or Clapinel, wrote a continuation extending the poem to 22,817 lines. The general story is of a visit to a garden of delights, on the outside of which are all unlovely things. Within the garden the personages and action are allegories of the art of love. Here are Leisure, Enjoyment, Courtesy, the God of Love himself, love in the form of a beautiful Rose, Gracious Reception, Guardianship, Coyness, and Reason. Our extracts are taken from the translation into English attributed—it now seems with great probability—to Chaucer.

NOTE.—These extracts from Chaucer's translation are not re-translated nor adapted. Chaucer's words are retained in every case. Their spelling is modernized. In those cases in which they needed for the rhythm, certain inflectional endings, e, en, es, are retained and are printed in parentheses. The reader has only to remember that he must pronounce every syllable needed to make the lines rhythmical. In only four cases has the rhyme been affected by the changed spelling. For defense of this modern spelling of Chaucer, the reader is referred to Lounsbury's "Studies in Chaucer," Vol. III., pp. 264-279.

Ll. 49-91.—
That it was May me thought(e) tho[1]
It is five year or more ago;
That it was May, thus dreamed me,
In time of love and jollity.
That all thing 'ginneth waxen gay,
For there is neither busk nor hay[2]
In May, that it nill[3] shrouded been
And [4] it with new(e) leaves wrene[5]
These wood(e)s eek recover green,
That dry in winter been to seen;[6]
And the earth waxeth proud withal
For sweet dews that on it fall.
And the poor estate forget

In which that winter had it set.
And then becometh the ground so proud,
That it will have a new(e) shroud,
And maketh so quaint his robe and fair
That it had hews an hundred pair,
Of grass and flowers, inde and perse[7]
And many hew(e)s full diverse:
That is the robe, I mean, ivis,[8]
Through which the ground to praise(n)[9] is.
The birds that have(n) left their song,
While they have suffered cold so strong,
In weathers grill [10] and dark to sight,
Ben [11] in May for [12] the sun(en) bright
So glad(e), that they show in singing
That in (t)heir hearts is such liking,[13]
That they mote [14] sing(en) and be light.
Then doth the nightingale her might
To make noise and sing(en) blithe,
Then is bussful many sithe,[15]
The calandra [16] and the popinjay.[17]
Then young(e) folk entend(en)[18] aye
For to be gay and amorous,
The time is then so favorous.[19]
Hard is the heart that loveth nought,
In May when all this mirth is wrought:
When he may on these branches hear
The small(e) bird(e)s sing(en) clear
(T)heir blissful' sweet song piteous,
And in this season delightous[20]
When love affrayeth[21] all(e) thing.

[1] Then. [2] Bush nor hedge. [3] Will not. [4] As if. [5] Were covered. [6] Are to be seen. [7] Azure and sky-colored. [8] Certainly. [9] To be praised. [10] Severe. [11] Are. [12] On account of. [13] Good bodily condition. [14] Must. [15] Times. [16] A kind of lark. [17] Parrot. [18] Attend. [19] Favorable. [20] Delightful. [21] Moveth.

The poet sees in vision the Garden of Love. He knocks at "a wiket smalle," which was finally opened by a maiden.

Ll. 539.—

Her hair was as yellow of hew
As any basin scoured new,
Her flesh tender as is a chick,
With bent brow(e)s, smooth and sleek;
And by measure large were,
The opening of her eyen [1]clere,
Her nose of good proportion,
Her eyen [1] gray as is a falcon,
With sweet(e) breath and well savored,
Her face white and well colored,
With little mouth and round to see;
A clove[2] chin eek had(de) she.
Her neek(e) was of good fashion[3]
In length and greatness by reason,[4]
Without(e) blain(e),[5] scab or roigne.[6]
From Jerusalem unto Burgoyne,
There nys [7] a fairer neck, iwis,[8]
To feel how smooth and soft it is.
Her throat also white of hew
As snow on branch(e) snowed new.
Of body full well wrought was she;
Men needed not in no country
A fairer body for to seek,

And of fine orphreys [9] had she eek
A chap(e)let; so seemly one,
Ne[10] I werede never maid upon,
And fair above that chap(e)let
A rose garland had she set.
She had a gay mirror,
And with a rich(e) gold treasure
Her head was tressed [11] quaint(e)ly;
Her sleeves sewed fetisely,[12]
And for to keep her hand(e)s fair
Of gloves white she had a pair.
And she had on a coat of green,
Of cloth of Gaunt; without(e) ween[13]
Well seemed by her apparel
She was not wont to great travail,
For when she kempto was fetisely[14]
And well arrayed and rich(e)ly
Then had she done all her journey;
For merry and well begun was she.
She had a lusty[15] life in May,
She had no thought by night nor day,
Of no thing but if it were only
To graith[16] her well and uncouthly.[17]
When that this door had opened me
This May, seemly for to see,
I thanked her as I best might,
And asked her how that she hight[18]
And what she was' I asked eek.
And she to me was nought unmeek [19]
Ne of her answer dangerous [20]
But fair answered and said(e) thus:
"Lo, sir, my name is Idleness;
So clepe[21] men me, more and less."

Full mighty and full rich am I,
And that of one thing, namely,"
For I entend(e)[28] to no thing
But to my joy, and my playing,
And for to kemb[29] and tress(e)[30] me.
Acquainted am I and privy
With Mirth(e), lord of this garden,
That from the land of Alexander
Made the trees hither be fet[31]
That in this garden be i-set.
And when the trees were waxen on height[32]
This wall, that stands here in thy sight,
Did Mirth enclose(n) all about;
And these images[33] all without
He did 'em both entail[43] and paint.
That neither be joly,[35] nor quaint,[36]
But they be full of sorrow and woe
As thou hast seen a while ago.
"And oft(e) time him to solace,
Sir Mirth(e) cometh into this place
And eek with him cometh his meiny[37]
That live in lust[38] and jollity,
And now is Mirth therein to hear
The bird(e)s, how they sing(en) clear
The mavis and the nightingale,
And other jolly bird(e)s small,
And thus he walketh to solace
Him and his folk; for sweeter place
To play(en) in he may not find,
Although he sought one in till[39] Inde.[40]
The alther fairest[41] folk to see
That in this world may found(e) be

Hath Mirth(e) with him in his rout,
That follow him always about.
. . . . .
And forth without(e) word(e)s mo,[42]
In at that wicket went I tho,[43]
That idleness had opened me,
Into that garden fair to see.

[1] Eyes. [2] Dimpled. [3] Form. [4] Proportion. [5] Pustule. [6] Pimple. [7] Is not. [8] Certainly. [9] Fringe of gold. [10] Not. [11] Wore. [12] Plaited. [13] Neatly. [14] Doubt. [15] Combed, ironed. [16] Day's work. [17] In fine form. [18] Pleasant. [19] Dress. [20] Unusually, elegantly. [21] Was called. [22] Bold. [23] Sparing. [24] Name. [25] Great and small. [26] Chiefly. [27] Attend. [29] Comb. [30] Plait. [31] Fetched. [32] Were grown to a height. [33] The pictures on the outside of the wall. [34] Scarve. [35] Joyful, pleasant. [36] Unusual, queer. [37] Retinue. [38] Pleasure. [39] To. [40] India. [41] Fairest of all. [42] More. [43] Then.

After wandering about the garden hearing the birds and getting acquainted with the inhabitants, he saw
Among a thousand thing(e)s mo[1]
A roser [2] charged full of roses,
That with an hedge about enclosed is.
Tho[3] had I such lust[4] and envy,
That for Paris nor for Pavie,
Nolde[5]I have left to go at see
There greatest heap of roses be.
When I was with this rage hent[6]
That caught hath many a man and shent[7]

Toward the roser I gan go.
And when I was not far therefro,[8]
The savor of the roses sweet
Me smote right to the heart(e) root
As I had all embalmed be.
And if I had ne[9] endoubted[10] me
To have been hated or assailed,
Me thank(e)s[11] would I not been failed
To pull a rose of all that rout,[12]
To bear(en) in my hand about
And smell(en) to it where I went;
But ever I dreaded me to repent,
And lest it grieved or forthought[13]
The lord that thilke[14] garden wrought,
Of roses there were great(e) wone,[15]
So fair(e) waxe [16] never in Rone.[17]
Of knop(e)s[18] close,[19] some saw I there
And some well better waxen[20] were,
And some there be of other moison[21]
That drew(e) nigh to their season,
And sped 'em fast(e) for to spread;
I love well such roses red;
For broad[22] roses, and open also,
Be passed in a day or two;
But knop(e)s[18] will(e) fresh(e) be
Two day(e)s at the least, or three,
The knop(e)s greatly liked[23]me,
For fairer may there no man see
Whoso might have one of all
It aught him be full lief[24]withall.
Might I one garland of 'em get
For no riches I would it let.[25]
Among the knop(e)s I chose one

So fair, that of the remnant none
Ne prize I half so well as it,
When I avise[26] it is my wit.
In it so well was enlumined
With color red, as well y-fined[27]
As nature couthe[28] it make fair.
And it had leaves well four pair,
That Kynde[29] hath set through his knowing
About the red roses springing.
The stalk(e) was as rush(e) right
And thereon stood the knop upright,
That it ne bowed upon no side,
The sweet(e) smell(e) sprang so wide
That it did[30] all the place about.
When I had smelled the savor sweet
No will had I from thence yet go
But somedeal[31] nearer it went I tho[32]
To take it: but mine hand for dread
Ne durst I to the rose bede[33]
For thistles sharp of many manners,
Nettles, thorns, and hooked briers;
For mickle they disturbed me,
For sore I dreaded to harmed be.

[1] More. [2] Rose-bush. [3] Then. [4] Desire. [5] Would not. [6] Seized. [7] Ruined. [8] There from. [9] Not. [10] Feared. [11] Willingly. [12] Company. [13] Caused to repent. [14] That. [15] Quantity. [16] Waxed, grew. [17] Provence. [18] Buds. [19] Closed. [20] Much better grown. [21] Harvest. [22] Blown.

[23] Pleased. [24] Pleasing. [25] Let go. [26] Consider.[27] Polished.

[28] Knew how. [29] Nature. [30] Filled. [31] Somewhat. [32] Then. [33] Offer.

CHAPTER II. SPANISH LITERATURE.

The golden age of Spanish literature embraces the sixteenth and seventeenth centuries; but the twelfth and thirteenth centuries were, in Spain as in other European countries, a period of special literary activity. The impulses at work were the same as those to be noted in contemporary France, England, and Germany, and the work produced of the same general types. The chief phases of Spanish mediaeval literature are these:

1. Epic and heroic poetry. Here, as elsewhere, heroic ballads grew up about the national heroes. These were gradually fused into long epic poems by the wandering minstrels. The best of these Chansons de Geste are (1) "The Poem of the Cid", (2) "Rhymed Chronicle of the Cid". Both of them belong probably to the twelfth century.

2. Romances. Many romances, or short semi-epic poems, grew up about the Cid. Of others, some were of the Carlovingian cycle, the most famous being that concerning Bernardo del Carpio, the traditional rival and conqueror of Roland. Some were devoted to the Arthurian legend. This latter cycle of stories was immensely popular in Spain, though rather in translation and imitation than in original

works. In the fourteenth century these older romances were technically called "books of chivalry" and their popularity and influence was widespread.

3. Lyric poetry. There seems to have been no special development of lyric poetry early in Spain, such as is found in France. The earliest noteworthy lyric poet is Juan Ruiz (1300-1350).

4. Didactic literature. As early as the first half of the thirteenth century, we have in Spain a strong didactic literature. Gonzalo de Berceo (d. 1268) wrote many lives of the saints, miracles, hymns to the Virgin, and other devotional pieces. But the impulse to allegorizing does not seem to come to Spain till much later.

5. Fables and tales. Though a little later in being developed in Spain than in France, the same delight was taken in fables and short tales. About the middle of the fourteenth century, Juan Manul (d. 1349) made, in his "El Conde Lucanor", a large collection of these tales.

6. Chronicles. Spain had early an excellent school of chroniclers. An example of their work is The General Chronicle of Spain, compiled under Alphonso the Wise (d. 1284).

ANCIENT BALLADS.

Romantic ballads grew up in the twelfth and thirteenth centuries in Spain, centering chiefly about the national hero, Rodrigo Diaz de Bivar, who was called THE CID, some account of whom is necessary in order to an understanding of the poems.

History—Rodrigo Diaz de Bivar, born 1030-40, died

1099, was the foremost warrior of the great struggle between the Christians and the Moors in Spain. The Moors called him the CID (Seid, the Lord), and the Champion (El Campeador). He was a vigorous, unscrupulous fighter, now on one side, now on the other. He was at one time entrusted with high embassies of state, at others, a rebel. His true place in history seems to be that of a great freebooter and guerrilla. His contemporary fame was really great.

Legend—During the lifetime of the CID many marvels and myths grew up about him, and within the next century they became almost numberless. He became the hero of poet and of romancer to the Spanish people. His story was told everywhere by the wandering minstrels, and his name became the center of all popular romances.

Literature.—At once, then, a large literature sprang up concerning the CID—ballads, romances, and incipient dramas. The chief pieces are (1)"The Ballads of the Cid", composed from the twelfth to the fifteenth century, of which nearly two hundred survive; (2)"The Poem of the Cid", a noble fragment; (3)"The Chronicle of the Cid".

The early history of Spain's popular hero is traced very accurately in (1)"The General Chronicle of Spain", compiled under Alphonso X. (died 1284); (2)"The Chronicle of the Cid", perhaps extracts from the first, and (3) Various Poems and Romances of the CID from the thirteenth to the fifteenth century.

The following give some of his adventures, and show the spirit of this interesting early literature—the earliest ballad literature in Europe.

From the Cid Ballads.

CUYDANDO DIEGO LAYNEZ. (THE TEST.)

Brooding sat Diego Laynez o'er the insult to his name,
Nobler and more ancient far than Inigo Abarca's fame;
For he felt that strength was wanting to avenge the craven blow,
If he himself at such an age to fight should think to go.
Sleepless he passed the weary nights, his food untasted lay,
Ne'er raised his eyes from off the ground, nor ventured forth to stray,
Refused all converse with his friends, impelled by mortal fear,
Lest fame of outrage unatoned should aggravate his care.
While pondering thus his honor's claims in search of just redress,
He thought of an expedient his failing house to test;
So summoning to his side his sons, excused all explanation,
Silent began to clutch their hands in proper alternation,
(Not by their tender palms to trace the chiromantic linings,
For at that day no place was found in Spain for such divinings),
But calling on his honor spent for strength and self-denial,
He set aside parental love and steeled his nerves to trial,
Griping their hands with all his might till each cried: "Hold, Sir, hold!
What meaneth this? pray, let me go; thou'rt killing me, behold!"
Now when he came to Roderick, the youngest of them all,
Despair had well-nigh banished hope of cherished fruit withal
(Though ofttimes lingering nearest when farthest thought

to be);
The young man's eyes flashed fury, like tiger fierce stood he
And cried: "Hold, father, hold, a curse upon ye, stay!
An ye were not my father, I would not stop to pray,
But by this good right arm of mine would straight pluck out your life
With a bare digit of my hand, in lieu of vulgar knife!
The old man wept for joy: "Son of my soul," quoth he,
"Thy rage my rage disarmeth, thine ire is good to see;
Prove now thy mettle, Rod'rick; wipe out my grievous stain,
Restore the honor I have lost, unless thou it regain—"
Then quickly told him of the wrong to which he was a prey,
Gave him his blessing and a sword and bade him go his way
To end the Count's existence and begin a brighter day.

— Tr. by Knapp.

PENSATIVO ESTAVA EL CID. (THE SOLILOQUY.)
Pensive stood the young Castilian, musing calmly on his plight;
'Gainst a man like Count Lozano to avenge a father's slight!
Thought of all the trained dependents that his foe could quickly call,
A thousand brave Asturians scattered through the highlands all;

Thought, too, how at the Cortes of Leon his voice prevailed,
And how in border forays the Moor before him quailed;
At last reviewed the grievance—No sacrifice too great
To vindicate the first affront to Layn Calvo's state;
Then calls on Heaven for justice, and on the earth for space,
Craves strength of honor injured, and of his father grace,
Nor heeds his youthful bearing, for men of rank like he
Are wont from birth to prove their worth by deeds of chivalry.

    Next from the wainscot took he down an ancient sword and long:
Once it had been Mudarra's, but now had rusty grown,
And, holding it sufficient to achieve the end he sought,
Before he girt it on him, he addressed the fitting thought:
"Consider, valiant claymore, that Mudarrals arm is mine,
And the cause wherein ye wrestle is Mudarra's cause and thine;
But if, forsooth, thou scornest to be grasped by youthful hand,
Think not 'twill lead thee backward e'en a jot from the demand;
For as firm as thine own steel thou wilt find me in the fray,
And as good as e'er the best man—Thou hast gained a lord to-day;
And if perchance they worst thee, enraged at such a stain,
I shall plunge thee to the cross in my breast for very shame.
Then on to the field away, for the hour to fight is come,
To requite on Count Lozano all the mischief he has done."
So, full of courage and emprise the Cid rode forth to war,
And his triumph was accomplished in the space of one

short hour.

— Tr. by KNAPP.

NON ES DE SESSUDOS HOMES. (ON THE FIELD).

"It is not meet for men of brain, nor yet for champion true,
To offer insult to a man of better blood than you!
The brawny warrior, howe'er fierce and valiant he may be,
Was never wont to test his power on aged infirmity.
The men of Leon need not boast of high emprise, forsooth,
Who craven smite the face of age, and not the breast of youth.
Ye should have known who was my sire, and Layn Calvo's line,
A breed that never brook offence, nor challenge fit decline;
How dared ye thus provoke a man whom only Heaven may,
And not another' while the son lives to avenge the day!
Ye cast about his noble face dishonor's sombre pall,
But I am here to strip it off and expiate it all;
For only blood will cleanse the stain attainted honor brings,
And valid blood is that alone which from the aggressor springs;
Yours it must be, Oh tyrant, since by its overplay
It moved ye to so foul a deed and robbed your sense away;
On my father ye laid hand, in the presence of the king,
And I, his son, am here to-day atonement fall to bring.
Count, ye did a craven business and I call ye COWARD here!
Behold, if I await you, think not I come with fear,

For Diego Laynez wrought me well set in his own mould,
And while I prove my birthright I your baseness shall unfold.
Your valor as a crafty blade will not avail ye more,
For to my needs I bring a sword and charger trained to war."
Thus spake to Count Lozano Spain's champion, the Cid,
(Ere long he won the title by achievements which he did)
That day he slew his enemy and severing quick the head,
Bore high the bleeding trophy as he homeward proudly sped.

— Tr. by Knapp.

LLORANDO DIEGO LAYNEZ. (THE TRIUMPH.)

Weeping sat Diego Laynez still o'er his untasted meal;
Still o'er his shame was brooding, the tears his thoughts reveal;
Beset with a thousand fancies, and crazed with honest care,
Sensitive to a footfall lest some foe were lurking there,
When Rod'rick, bearing by the locks the Count's dissevered poll,
Tracking the floor with recent gore, advanced along the hall.
He touched his father's shoulder and roused him from his dream,
And proudly flaunting his revenge he thus addresses him:
"Behold the evil tares, sir, that ye may taste the wheat;
Open thine eyes, my father, and lift thy head, 'tis meet,
For this thine honor is secure, is raised to life once more,
And all the stain is washed away in spite of pride and

power:
For here are hands that are not hands, this tongue no tongue is
now,
I have avenged thee, sir, behold, and here the truth avow."
The old man thinks he dreams; but no, no dream is there;
'Twas only his long grieving that had filled his heart with care.
At length he lifts his eyes, spent by chivalrous deeds,
And turns them on his enemy clad in the ghastly weeds:
"Roderick, son of my soul, mantle the spectre anon,
Lest, like a new Medusa, it change my heart to stone,
And leave me in such plight at last, that, ere I wish ye joy,
My heart should rend within me of bliss without alloy.
Oh, infamous Lozano! kind heaven hath wrought redress,
And the great justice of my claim hath fired Rodrigo's breast!
Sit down, my son, and dine, here at the head with me,
For he who bringest such a gift, is head of my family."

— Tr. by Knapp.

THE YOUNG CID.

Now rides Diego Laynez, to kiss the good King's hand,
Three hundred men of gentry go with him from his land,
Among them, young Rodrigo, the proud Knight of Bivar;
The rest on mules are mounted, he on his horse of war.

They ride in glittering gowns of soye—He harnessed like a lord;

There is no gold about the boy, but the crosslet of his sword;
The rest have gloves of sweet perfume,—He gauntlets strong of
mail;
They broidered cap and flaunting plume,—He crest untaught to
quail.

All talking with each other thus along their way they passed,
But now they've come to Burgos, and met the King at last;
When they came near his nobles, a whisper through them ran,—
"He rides amidst the gentry that slew the Count Lozan."

With very haughty gesture Rodrigo reined his horse,
Right scornfully he shouted, when he heard them so discourse,
"If any of his kinsmen or vassals dare appear,
The man to give them answer, on horse or foot, is here."—

"The devil ask the question," thus muttered all the band;—
With that they all alighted, to kiss the good King's hand,—
All but the proud Rodrigo, he in his saddle stayed,—
Then turned to him his father (you may hear the words he said).

"Now, light, my son, I pray thee, and kiss the good King's hand,
He is our lord, Rodrigo; we hold of him our land."—
But when Rodrigo heard him, he looked in sulky sort,
I wot the words he answered they were both cold and short.

"Had any other said it, his pains had well been paid,
But thou, sir, art my father, thy word must be obeyed."—
With that he sprung down lightly, before the King to kneel,
But as the knee was bending, out leapt his blade of steel.

The King drew back in terror, when he saw the sword was bare;
"Stand back, stand back, Rodrigo, in the devil's name beware;
Your looks bespeak a creature of father Adam's mould,
But in your wild behaviour you're like some lion bold."

When Rodrigo heard him say so, he leapt into his seat,
And thence he made his answer, with visage nothing sweet,—
"I'd think it little honour to kiss a kingly palm,
And if my father's kissed it, thereof ashamed I am."—

When he these words had uttered, he turned him from the gate.
His true three hundred gentles behind him followed straight;
If with good gowns they came that day, with better arms they went;
And if their mules behind did stay, with horses they're content.

— Tr. by Lockhart.

THE CID'S COURTSHIP.

Now, of Rodrigo de Bivar great was the fame that run,
How he five Kings had vanquished, proud Moormen every one;
And how, when they consented to hold of him their ground,
He freed them from the prison wherein they had been bound.

To the good King Fernando, in Burgos where he lay,
Came then Ximena Gomez, and thus to him did say:—
"I am Don Gomez, daughter, in Gormaz Count was he;
Him slew Rodrigo of Bivar in battle valiantly.

"Now am I come before you, this day a boon to crave,

And it is that I to husband may this Rodrigo have;
Grant this, and I shall hold me a happy damosell,
Much honoured shall I hold me, I shall be married well.

"I know he's born for thriving, none like him in the land;
I know that none in battle against his spear may stand;
Forgiveness is well pleasing in God our Saviour's view,
And I forgive him freely, for that my sire he slew."—

Right pleasing to Fernando was the thing she did propose;
He writes his letter swiftly, and forth his foot-page goes;
I wot, when young Rodrigo saw how the King did write,
He leapt on Bavieca—I wot his leap was light.

With his own troop of true men forthwith he took the way,
Three hundred friends and kinsmen, all gently born were they;
All in one colour mantled, in armour gleaming gay,
New were both scarf and scabbard, when they went forth that day.

The King came out to meet him with words of hearty cheer;

Quoth he, "My good Rodrigo, you are right welcome here;
This girl Ximena Gomez would have ye for her lord,
Already for the slaughter her grace she doth accord.

"I pray you be consenting, my gladness will be great;
You shall have lands in plenty, to strengthen your estate."
"Lord King", Rodrigo answers, "in this and all beside,
Command, and I'll obey you. The girl shall be my bride."—

But when the fair Ximena came forth to plight her hand,
Rodrigo, gazing on her, his face could not command:
He stood and blushed before her;—thus at the last said he —

"I slew thy sire, Ximena, but not in villany:-

"In no disguise I slew him, man against man I stood;
There was some wrong between us* and I did shed his blood.
I slew a man, I owe a man; fair lady, by God's grace,
An honoured husband thou shalt have in thy dead father's place."

[1] See the account of this quarrel, "Non es de Sessudos Homes."

— Tr. by Lockhart.

BAVIECA.

The favorite warrior horse of the Cid. There are several more ballads devoted to this charger.

The King looked on him kindly, as on a vassal true;
Then to the King Ruy Diaz spake after reverence due,—
"O King, the thing is shameful, that any man beside
The liege lord of Castile himself should Bavieca ride:

"For neither Spain or Araby could another charger bring
So good as he, and certes, the best befits my King.
But that you may behold him, and know him to the core,
I'll make him go as he was wont when his nostrils smelt the Moor."

With that, the Cid, clad as he was in mantle furred and wide,
On Bavieca vaulting, put the rowel in his side;
And up and down, and round and round, so fierce was his career,
Streamed like a pennon on the wind Ruy Diaz' minivere.

And all that saw them praised them—they lauded man and horse,
As matched well, and rivalless for gallantry and force
Ne'er had they looked on horseman might to this knight come near,

Nor on other charger worthy of such a cavalier.

Thus, to and fro a-rushing, the fierce and furious steed,
He snapt in twain his hither rein:—"God pity now the Cid."
"God pity Diaz," cried the Lords,—but when they looked again,
They saw Ruy Diaz ruling him, with the fragment of his rein;
They saw him proudly ruling with gesture firm and calm,
Like a true lord commanding—and obeyed as by a lamb.

And so he led him foaming and panting to the King,
But "No," said Don Alphonso, "it were a shameful thing
That peerless Bavieca should ever be bestrid
By any mortal but Bivar—Mount, mount again, my Cid."

— Tr. by Lockhart.

FROM THE POEM OF THE CID.

The Cid has been banished by King Alphonso, has entered the Moors, country and taken a city. The Moors rally, gather their allies and surround the Cid's army. He turns to consult with his men.

"From water they have cut us off, our bread is running low;
If we would steal away by night, they will not let us go;
Against us there are fearful odds if we make choice to fight;
What would ye do now gentlemen, in this our present

plight?"
Minaya was the first to speak: said the stout cavalier,
"Forth from Castile the gentle thrust, we are but exiles here;
Unless we grapple with the Moor bread he will never yield;
A good six hundred men or more we have to take the field;
In God's name let us falter not, nor countenance delay,
But sally forth and strike a blow upon to-morrow's day."
"Like thee the counsel," said my Cid; "thou speakest to my mind;
And ready to support thy word thy hand we ever find."
Then all the Moors that bide within the walls he bids to go
Forth from the gates, lest they, perchance, his purpose come to
know
In making their defences good they spend the day and night,
And at the rising of the sun they arm them for the fight.
Then said the Cid: "Let all go forth, all that are in our band;
Save only two of those on foot, beside the gate to stand.
Here they will bury us if death we meet on yonder plain,
But if we win our battle there, rich booty we shall gain.
And thou Pero Bermuez, this my standard thou shalt hold;
It is a trust that fits thee well, for thou art stout and bold;
But see that thou advance it not unless I give command."
Bermuez took the standard and he kissed the Champion's hand.
Then bursting through the castle gates upon the plain they is
how;
Back on their lines in panic fall the watchmen of the foe.
And hurrying to and fro the Moors are arming all around,

While Moorish drums go rolling like to split the very ground,
And in hot haste they mass their troops behind their standards
twain,
Two mighty bands of men-at-arms to count them it were vain.
And now their line comes sweeping on, advancing to the fray,
Sure of my Cid and all his band to make an easy prey.
"Now steady, comrades'" said my Cid; "our ground we have to
stand;
Let no man stir beyond the ranks until I give command."
Bermuez fretted at the word, delay he could not brook;
He spurred his charger to the front, aloft the banner shook:
"O loyal Cid Campeador, God give the aid! I go
To plant thy ensign in among the thickest of the foe;
And ye who serve it, be it yours our standard to restore."
"Not so—as thou dost love me, stay!" called the Campeador.
Came Pero's answer, "Their attack I cannot, will not stay."
He gave his horse the spur and dashed against the Moors array.
To win the standard eager all the Moors await the shock,
Amid a rain of blows he stands unshaken as a rock.
Then cried my Cid: "In charity, on to the rescue—ho!"
With bucklers braced before their breasts, with lances pointing
low,
With stooping crests and heads bent down above the saddle bow,
All firm of hand and high of heart they roll upon the foe.
And he that in a good hour was born, his clarion voice

rings out,
And clear above the clang of arms is heard his battle shout,
"Among them, gentlemen! Strike home for the love of charity!
The Champion of Bivar is here—Ruy Diaz—I am he!"
Then bearing where Bermuez still maintains unequal fight,
Three hundred lances down they come, their pennons flickering
white;
Down go three hundred Moors to earth, a man to every blow;
And when they wheel three hundred more, as wheeling back they go.
It was a sight to see the lances rise and fall that day;
The shivered shields and riven mail, to see how thick they lay;
The pennons that went in snow-white come out a gory red;
The horses running riderless, the riders lying dead;
While Moors call on Mohammed, and "St. James!" the Christians
cry,
And sixty score of Moors and more in narrow compass lie.
Above his gilded saddle-bow there played the Champion's sword;
And Minaya Alvar Fanez, Zurita's gallant lord;
Add Martin Antolinez the worthy Burgalese;
And Muno Gustioz his squire—all to the front were these.
And there was Martin Mufloz, he who ruled in Mont Mayor;
And there was Alvar Alvarez, and Alvar Salvador;
And the good Galin Garcia, stout lance of Arragon;
And Felix Mufloz, nephew of my Cid the Champion.

Well did they quit themselves that day, all these and many more,
In rescue of the standard for my Cid Campeador.

— Tr. by Ormsby.

THE BATTLE WITH KING BUCAR OF MOROCCO, AT VALENCIA.

Loud from among the Moorish tents the call to battle comes,
And some there are, unused to war, awed by the rolling drums.
Ferrando and Diego most: of troubled mind are they;
Not of their will they find themselves before the Moors that day.
"Pero Burmuez," said the Cid, "my nephew staunch and true,
Ferrando and Diego do I give in charge to you;
Be yours the task in this day's fight my sons-in-law to shield,
For, by God's grace to-day we sweep the Moors from off the
field!"
"Nay," said Bermuez, "Cid, for all the love I bear to thee,
The safety of thy sons-in-law no charge of mine shall be.
Let him who will the office fill; my place is at the front,
Among the comrades of my choice to bear the battle's brunt;
As it is thine upon the rear against surprise to guard,
And ready stand to give support where'er the fight goes hard."

Came Alvar Fanez: "Loyal Cid Campeador," he cried,
"This battle surely God ordains—He will be on our side;
Now give the order of attack which seems to thee the befit,
And, trust me, every man of us will do his chief's behest."
But lo! all armed from head to heel the Bishop Jeronie shows;
He ever brings good fortune to my Cid where'er he goes.
"Mass have I said, and now I come to join you in the fray;
To strike a blow against the Moor in battle if I may,
And in the field win honor for my order and my hand.
It is for this that I am here, far from my native land.
Unto Valencia did I come to cast my lot with you,
All for the longing that I had to slay a Moor or two.
And so in warlike guise I come, with blazoned shield and lance,
That I may flesh my blade to-day, if God but give the chance,
Then send me to the front to do the bidding of my heart:
Grant me this favor that I ask, or else, my Cid, we part."
"Good!" said my Cid. "Go, flesh thy blade; there stand thy Moorish
foes.
Now shall we see how gallantly our fighting Abbot goes."
He said; and straight the Bishop's spurs are in his charger's flanks,
And with a will he flings himself against the Moorish ranks.
By his good fortune, and the aid of God, that loved him well,
Two of the foe before his point at the first onset fell.
His lance he broke, he drew his sword—God! how the good steel
played!
Two with the lance he slew, now five go down beneath his

blade.
But many are the Moors and round about him fast they close,
And on his hauberk, and his shield, they rain a shower of blows.
He in the good hour born beheld Don Jerome sorely pressed;
He braced his buckler on his arm, he laid his lance in rest,
And aiming where beset by Moors the Bishop stood at bay,
Touched Bavieca with the spur and plunged into the fray;
And flung to earth unhorsed were seven, and lying dead were four,
Where breaking through the Moorish ranks came the Campeador.
God it so pleased, that this should be the finish of the fight;
Before the lances of my Cid the fray became a flight;
And then to see the tent-ropes burst, the tent-poles prostrate
flung!
As the Cid's horsemen crashing came the Moorish tents among.
Forth from the camp King Bucar's Moors they drove upon the plain,
And charging on the rout, they rode and cut them down amain
Here severed lay the mail-clad arm, there lay the steel-capped
head,
And here the charger riderless, ran trampling on the dead.
Behind King Bucar as he fled my Cid came spurring on;
"Now, turn thee, Bucar, turn!" he cried; "here is the Bearded One:

Here is that Cid you came to seek, King from beyond the main,
Let there be peace and amity to-day between us twain."
Said Bucar, "Nay; thy naked sword, thy rushing steed, I see;
If these mean amity, then God confound such amity.
Thy hand and mine shall never join unless in yonder deep,
If the good steed that I bestride his footing can but keep."
Swift was the steed, but swifter borne on Bavieca's stride,
Three fathoms from the sea my Cid rode at King Bucar's side;
Aloft his blade a moment played, then on the helmet's crown,
Shearing the steel-cap dight with gems, Colada he brought down.
Down to the belt, through helm and mail, he cleft the Moor in
twain.
And so he slew King Bucar, who came from beyond the main.
This was the battle, this the day, when he the great sword won,
Worth a full thousand marks of gold—the famous Brand Tizon.

— Tr. by Ormsby.

CHAPTER III.
SCANDINAVIAN LITERATURE.

Scandinavian literature embraces the literature of Norway, Sweden, Iceland, and their western colonies. In the Middle Ages this literature reached its fullest and best development in Iceland.

The earliest and greatest portion of this literature is the heroic poetry forming the collection called the Poetic or Elder Edda. Like all early poetry these were minstrel poems, passing orally from singer (skald) to singer for centuries. Some of them were composed as early as the eighth century. The collection was probably made in the thirteenth century (1240). The collection consists of thirty-nine distinct songs or poems. They are based upon common Norse mythology and tradition. In one section of this collection is found in outline the story of the Nibelungs and Brunhild-the story which later formed the basis of the

"Niebelungen-Lied". This fact connects the two literatures with the original common Teutonic traditions. Anderson says, "The Elder Edda presents the Norse cosmogony, the doctrines of the Odinic mythology, and the lives and doings of the gods. It contains also a cycle of poems on the demigods and mythic heroes and heroines of the same period. It gives us as complete a view of the mythological world of the North as Homer and Hesiod do of that of Greece" (Norse Mythology). Almost equal in importance and interest is the Prose Edda, sometimes called the Younger Edda, arranged and in part written by Snorra Sturleson, who lived from 1178 to 1241. The chief portions of it are:

1. "Gylfaginning," in which Odin recounts to Gylf the history of the gods.

2. "Bragaraethur, the conversations of Braga the god of poetry.

Other and less important varieties of Scandinavian literature are the romances of history and romances of pure fiction.

VOLUSPA. THE ORACLE OF THE PROPHETESS VALA.

The Voluspa is the first song in the Elder Edda. It is a song of a prophetess and gives an account of the creation of the world, of man, giants, and dwarfs; of the employments of fairies or destinies; of the functions of the gods, their adventures, their quarrels, and the vengeance they take; of the final state of the universe and its dissolution; of the battle of the lower deities and the evil beings; of the renovation of the world; of the happy lot of the good, and the punishment of the wicked. The first passage selected gives the account of creation.

> In early times,
> When Ymer[1] lived,
> Was sand, nor sea,
> Nor cooling wave;
> No earth was found,
> Nor heaven above;
> One chaos all,
> And nowhere grass:
>
> Until Bor's[2] sons
> Th' expanse did raise,
> By whom Midgard [3]
> The great was made.
> From th' south the sun
> Shone on the walls;
> Then did the earth
> Green herbs produce.
>
> The sun turned south;
> The moon did shine;
> Her right hand held
> The horse of heaven.
> The sun knew not
> His proper sphere;
> The stars knew not
> Their proper place;
> The moon know not

Her proper power.

    Then all the powers
Went to the throne,
The holy gods,
And held consult:
Night and cock-crowing
Their names they gave,
Morning also,
And noon-day tide,
And afternoon,
The years to tell.

    The Asas[4] met
On Ida's plains,
Who altars raised
And temples built;
Anvils they laid,
And money coined;
Their strength they tried
In various ways,
When making songs,
And forming tools.

On th' green they played
In joyful mood,
Nor knew at all
The want of gold,
Until there came
Three Thursa maids,
Exceeding strong,
From Jotunheim:[5]

. . . .

Until there came
Out of the ranks,
Powerful and fair,
Three Asas home,
And found on shore,
In helpless plight,
Ask and Embla [6]
Without their fate.

They had not yet
Spirit or mind,
Blood, or beauty,
Or lovely hue.
Odin gave spirit,
Heinir gave mind,
Lothur gave blood
And lovely hue.

[1] Ymer, the progenitor of the giants.

[2] Bor, the father of Odin, Vile, and Ve.

[3] Midgard, the earth.

[4] Asas, the gods.

[5] The home of the giants.

[6] The first man and first woman made out of pine trees by the three gods Odin, Heinir, and Lothur.

— Tr. by Henderson.

The second passage gives an account of the universal dissolution—called Ragnarok, the Twilight of the Gods.

Loud barks Garm 1]
At Gnipa-cave;
The fetters are severed,
The wolf is set free,
Vala[2] knows the future.
More does she see
Of the victorious gods,
Terrible fall.

From the east drives Hrym,[3]
Bears his child before him;
Jormungander welters
In giant fierceness;
The waves thunder;
The eagle screams,
Rends the corpses with pale beak,
And Naglfar[4] is launched.
A ship from the east nears,
The hosts of Muspel
Come o'er the main,

But Loke is pilot.
All grim and gaunt monsters
Conjoin with the wolf,
And before them all goes
The brother of Byleist.[5]

    From the south wends Surt [6]
With seething fire;
The sun of the war-god
Shines in his sword;
Mountains together dash,
And frighten the giant-maids;
Heroes tread the paths to Hel,
And heaven in twain is rent.
Over Him [7] then shall come
Another woe,
When Odin goes forth
The wolf to combat.
. . . .
All men
Abandon the earth.

    The sun darkens,
The earth sinks into the ocean;
The lucid stars
From heaven vanish;
Fire and vapor
Rage toward heaven;
High flames

Involve the skies.

    Loud barks Garm
At Gnipa-eave:
The fetters are severed,
The wolf is set free,—
Vala knows the future.
More does she see
Of the victorious gods,
Terrible fall.

    [1] Hel's dog.

    [2] Vala, the prophetess.

    [3] The winter.

    [4] Naglfar, a ship of the gods.

    [5] The brother of Byleist, Loke.

    [6] Surt, a fire-giant.

    [7] Hlin, a name sometimes used for the goddess, Frigg.

— Tr. by Thorpe.
    The conclusion of the "Voluspa" is the following picture of the regenerated earth.
    She sees arise,
The second time,
From the sea, the earth
Completely green:

Cascades do fall;
The eagle soars,
That on the hills
Pursues his prey.

    The gods convene
On Ida's plains,
And talk of man,
The worm of dust:
They call to mind
Their former might,
And the ancient runes
Of Fimbultyr.[1]

    The fields unsown
Shall yield their growth;
All ills shall cease;
Balder[2] shall come,
And dwell with Hauthr[3]
In Hropt's[4] abodes.
Say, warrior-gods,
Conceive ye yet?

    A hall she sees
Outshine the sun,
Of gold its roof,
It stands in heaven:
The virtuous there

Shall always dwell,
And evermore
Delights enjoy.

[1] Fimbultyr, Odin.

[2] Balder, the god of the summer.

[3] Hauthr, Hoder, the brother of Balder.

[4] Hropt, Odin. of Odinic morality and precepts of wisdom, in the form of social and moral maxims.

— Tr. by Henderson.

HAVAMAL.

The High-Song of Odin. This is the second song in the Elder Edda. Odin himself is represented as its author. It contains a pretty complete code.

All door-ways
Before going forward,
Should be looked to;
For difficult it is to know
Where foes may sit
Within a dwelling.
. . . .
Of his understanding
No one should be proud,
But rather in conduct cautious.
When the prudent and taciturn
Come to a dwelling,
Harm seldom befalls the cautious;

For a firmer friend
No man ever gets
Than great sagacity.

. . . .

One's own house is best,
Small though it be;
At home is every one his own master.
Though he but two goats possess,
And a straw-thatched cot,
Even that is better than begging.

    One's own house is best,
Small though it be;
At home is every one his own master.
Bleeding at heart is he
Who has to ask
For food at every meal-tide.

. . . .

A miserable man,
And ill-conditioned,
Sneers at everything:
One thing he knows not,
Which he ought to know,
That he is not free from faults.

. . . .

Know if thou hast a friend
Whom thou fully trustest,
And from whom thou would'st good derive;
Thou should'st blend thy mind with his,
And gifts exchange,
And often go to see him.

    If thou hast another
Whom thou little trustest,
Yet would'st good from him derive,
Thou should'st speak him fair,
But think craftily,
And leasing pay with lying.

    But of him yet further
Whom thou little trustest,
And thou suspectest his affection,
Before him thou should'st laugh,
And contrary to thy thoughts speak;
Requital should the gift resemble.

    I once was young,
I was journeying alone
And lost my way;
Rich I thought myself
When I met another:
Man is the joy of man.

    Liberal and brave
Men live best,
They seldom cherish sorrow;
But a bare-minded man

Dreads everything;
The niggardly is uneasy even at gifts.

    My garments in a field
I gave away
To two wooden men:
Heroes they seemed to be
When they got cloaks:[1]
Exposed to insult is a naked man.
. . . . .
Something great
Is not always to be given,
Praise is often for a trifle bought.
With half a loaf
And a tilted vessel
I got myself a comrade.
Little are the sand grains,
Little the wits,
Little the minds of men;
For all men
Are not wise alike:
Men are everywhere by halves.
Moderately wise
Should each one be,
But never over-wise;
For a wise man's heart
Is seldom glad,
If he is all-wise who owns it.
. . . .
Much too early
I came to many places,

But too late to others;
The beer was drunk, or not ready:
The disliked seldom hits the moment.
. . . .
Cattle die,
Kindred die,
We ourselves also die;
But the fair fame
Never dies of him who has earned it.

    Cattle die,
Kindred die,
We ourselves also die;
But I know one thing
That never dies,
Judgment on each one dead.

    [1] The tailor makes the man.

    — Tr. by Thorpe.

VAFTHRUDNISMAL. THE SONG OF VAFTHRUD-NER.

From the third poem in the Elder Edda came the following lines, describing the day and the night:

    Delling called is he
Who the Day's father is,
But Night was of Norve born;
The new and waning moons
The beneficent powers created

To count years for men.

    Skinfaxe[1] he is named
That the bright day draws
Forth over human kind;
Of coursers he is best accounted
Among faring men;
Ever sheds light that horse's mane.

    Hrimfaxe[2] he is called
That each night draws forth
Over the beneficent powers;
He from his bit lets fall
Drops every morn
Whence in the dells comes dew.
—Tr. by Thorpe

[1] Skinfaxe (shining mane), the horse of Day.

[2] Hrimfaxe (Rime mane), the horse of Night.

CHAPTER IV. GERMAN LITERATURE.

There are three classical periods in German literature.[1]

[1] See Scherer's "History of German Literature." Vol. I., page 16.

1. The Old High German Period, culminating about 600 A. D. The chief development of this period is the epic legend and poetry. As this literature remained largely unwritten, it is all lost except one fragment, The Song of Hildebrand.

2. The Middle High German Period, culminating about 1200 A. D. This was in Germany, as elsewhere in Europe, a time of abundant literary activity. It is the period of the renaissance of the heroic legends of the first period, and their remaking into developed epic poetry; of the writing of romances of chivalry and of antiquity; of the development of the lyric poetry of the Minnesingers; of the growth of popular fables and tales and of the drama. In short, all the forms of literary production known to the Middle Ages flourished in Germany in this period.

3. The Modern Classical Period, culminating about

1800 in the work of Goethe, Schiller, and the many poets and scholars surrounding them.

THE NATIONAL EPIC.

The fragment of the "Song of Hildebrand" is the sole surviving portion of the heroic literature of the first period. The story runs that "Hildebrand had fought in his youth in Italy, married there, and left a three-year son, when he was driven by Odoacer to Attila, king of the Huns. After years, in which the son grew up to manhood, Hildebrand re-entered Italy as a great chief in the army of Theodorle. His son, Hadubrand was then a chief combatant in Odoacer's army." They challenge each other to combat, and though the fragment ends before the fight is over, it is thought from other references that Hildebrand is victor.

THE SONG OF HILDEBRAND.

I have heard tell, they called each other forth,
Hildebrand, Hadubrand, among the hosts.
Son, father, made them ready for the strife.
Donned their war shirts, and girded on their swords
Over ringed mail, rode, heroes, to the fight.

Hildebrand, Herbrand's son, the elder man
And wiser, spake, well skilled in questionings
Asked in few words, who among all the folk
His father was, "or of what stock thou be?
Tell, and I'll give a mail of triple web:
Child in this realm, I knew its families."
Hadubrand spoke, Hildebrand's son: "The old
And wise among our folk tell me my father

Was Hildebrand, my name is Hadubrand.
My father went to the east to fly the hate
Of Otaker, with Dietrich and his bands.
A slender bride abiding in the lands
He left in bower, with an ungrown child,
And weapons masterless. Eastward he went
When sorrow came to Deitrich, friendless man,
My kinsman Otaker became his foe.
Most famed of warriors, since Dietrich fell,
Foremost in every field, he loved the fight,
Praised by the bold, I doubt not he is dead."

"Lord God of men," spake Hildebrand, "from heaven
Stay strife between two men so near in blood!"
Then twisted from his arm the bracelet ring
That once the King of Huns had given him,
I give it you in token of my love."
Spake Hadubrand, the son of Hildebrand,
"At the spear's point I take of you such gifts,
Point against point. No comrade thou, old Hun,
With Bly, enticing words wouldst win me near:
My answer to thee is with cast of spear.
Thou'rt old. This cunning out of age is bred."
Over the Midland Sea came foes who said,
"Hildebrand, son of Herbrand, he is dead."

Hildebrand, son of Herbrand, spake again:
"Thine arms show that in this land thou couldst not gain
A liberal leader or a royal friend.

Now well away. Great God, fate's evil end!
For sixty years, exile in stranger lands,
Summer and winter with spear-darting bands,
Never once leg bound within city wall,
I come back by my own son's hand to fall,
Hewn by his sword, or be his murderer,—
But if thy strength hold, thou canst readily
Win of the brave his arms, spoil of the slain,
When thine by right." Said Hildebrand, "Now, worst
Of Ostrogoths be he who holds me back! My heart is for the fray.
Judge comrades who look on, which of us wins
The fame, best throws the dart, and earns the spoil."
The ashen spears then sped, stuck in the shields
With their keen points, and down on the white shields
The heavy axes rang with sounding blows,
Shattering their rims, the flesh behind stood firm....

— Tr. by Morley.

In the second, or Middle High German Period, the heroic legends of early times were revived and formed the subject matter of many epic and semi epic poems. These legends have been classified into six several cycles of romances:[1]

[1] Cf. Morley's "English Writers." Vol. III., pp. 152-4.

1. The Frankish cycle contains the stories of Siegfried, the Sigurd of the Scandinavian tradition.

2. The Burgundian cycle contains King Gunther.

3. The Ostrogoth cycle contains Dietrich, Theodoric,

and Hildebrand.

4. The Hungarian cycle, to which belongs Attila or Etzel, and Rudiger.

5. The Lombard cycle, to which belong King Rother, King Otnit, and Wolfdietrich.

6. The North Saxon cycle, to which belongs the tale of Gudrun. The two most important of all the epics based upon these cycles are the Gudrun and the Niebelungenlied. The latter is the more comprehensive, national, and famous. It includes and unifies all the tales from the first four cycles of heroic legends.[1] The whole of German art, literature, and tradition is full of reflections of this poem. The best scholarship has concluded that the poem is not the work of a single author, but, like other folk epics, an edited collection of songs. The work was finished about 1190-1210. It consists of two greater parts, (1) the "Death of Siegfried" and (2) the "Vengeance of Kriemhild".

[1] See Kluge, "Geschichte der Deutschen National-Literature," p. 33.

From the "Niebelungenlied". The first song in the poem gives us
Kriemhild's foreboding dream.

KRIEMHILD'S DREAM.
Stanzas 1-19.

In stories of our fathers high marvels we are told
Of champions well approved in perils manifold.

Of feasts and merry meetings, of weeping and of wail,
And deeds of gallant daring I'll tell you in my tale.

    In Burgundy there flourish'd a maid so fair to see,
That in all the world together a fairer could not be.
This maiden's name was Kriemhild; through her in dismal strife
Full many a proudest warrior thereafter lost his life.

    Many a fearless champion, as such well became,
Woo'd the lovely lady; she from none had blame.
Matchless was her person, matchless was her mind.
This one maiden's virtue grac'd all womankind.

    Three puissant Kings her guarded with all the care they might,
Gunther and eke Gernot, each a redoubted knight,
And Giselher the youthful, a chosen champion he;
This lady was their sister, well lov'd of all the three.

    They were high of lineage, thereto mild of mood,
But in field and foray champions fierce and rude.
They rul'd a mighty kingdom, Burgundy by name;
They wrought in Etzel's country deeds of deathless fame.

At Worms was their proud dwelling, the fair Rhine flowing by,
There had they suit and service from haughtiest chivalry
For broad lands and lordships, and glorious was their state,
Till wretchedly they perish'd by two noble ladies' hate.

Dame Uta was their mother, a queen both rich and sage;
Their father hight Dancrat, who the fair heritage
Left to his noble children when he his course had run;
He too by deeds of knighthood in youth had worship won.

Each of these three princes, as you have heard me say,
Were men of mighty puissance. They had beneath their sway
The noblest knights for liegemen that ever dwelt on ground;
For hardihood and prowess were none so high renown'd.

There was Hagan of Troy of a noble line,
His brother nimble Dankwart, and the knight of Metz, Ortwine,
Eckewart and Gary, the margraves stout in fight,
Folker of Alzeia, full of manly might.

Rumolt the steward (a chosen knight was he),

Sindolt, and Hunolt; these serv'd the brethren three,
At their court discharging their several duties well;
Besides, knights had they many whom now I cannot tell.

Dankwart was marshal to the king his lord,
Ortwine of Metz, his nephew, was carver at the board,
Sindolt he was butler, a champion choice and true,
The chamberlain was Hunolt; they well their duties knew.

The gorgeous pomp and splendour, wherein these brethren reign'd,
How well they tended knighthood, what worship they attain'd,
How they thro' life were merry, and mock'd at woe and bale—
Who'd seek all this to tell you, would never end his tale.

A dream was dreamt by Kriemhild the virtuous and the gay,
How a wild young falcon she train'd for many a day,
Till two fierce eagles tore it; to her there could not be
In all the world such sorrow at this perforce to see.
To her mother Uta at once the dream she told,

But she the threatening future could only thus unfold;
"The falcon that thou trainedst is sure a noble mate;

God shield him in his mercy, or thou must lose him straight."

"A mate for me? what say'st thou, dearest mother mine?
Ne'er to love, assure thee, my heart will I resign.
I'll live and die a maiden, and end as I began,
Nor (let what else befall me) will suffer woe for man."

"Nay", said her anxious mother, "renounce not marriage so;
Wouldst thou true heartfelt pleasure taste ever here below,
Man's love alone can give it. Thou'rt fair as eye can see,
A fitting mate God send thee, and nought will wanting be."

"No more," the maiden answer'd, "no more, dear mother, say;
From many a woman's fortune this truth is clear as day,
That falsely smiling Pleasure with Pain requites us ever.
I from both will keep me, and thus will sorrow never."

So in her lofty virtues, fancy-free and gay,
Liv'd the noble maiden many a happy day,
Nor one more than another found favour in her sight;
Still at the last she wedded a far-renowned knight.

He was the self-same falcon she in her dream had seen,
Foretold by her wise mother. What vengeance took the queen
On her nearest kinsmen who him to death had done!
That single death atoning died many a mother's son.

In his home in the Netherlands the hero Siegfried hears of the beauty of Kriemhild and after magnificent preparations comes to Worms to win her, if possible, for his bride. After a long stay at the court of her brother, he finally sees her at a feast. They love each other at their first meeting. In Isenstein, far over the sea, lives Brunhild, the Amazon-queen, who is pledged to wed only him who can conquer her in single combat. Gunther, the brother of Kriemhild, desires her for his wife. Siegfried promises to win her for him on condition that Gunther grant him Kriemhild's hand in return. They proceed to Brunhild's land, where Siegfried, by the aid of a magic cloak, which renders him invisible, helps Gunther to overcome Brunhild.

THE CONQUEST OF BRUNHILD.
Stanza 447-455.

There too was come fair Brunhild; arm'd might you see her stand,
As though resolv'd to champion all kings for all their land.
She bore on her silk surcoat, gold spangles light and thin,
That quivering gave sweet glimpses of her fair snowy skin.

Then came on her followers, and forward to the field
Of ruddy gold far-sparkling bore a mighty shield,
Thick, and broad, and weighty, with studs of steel o'erlaid,
The which was wont in battle to wield the martial maid.

As thong to that huge buckler a gorgeous band there lay;
Precious stones beset it as green as grass in May;
With varying hues it glitter'd against the glittering gold.
Who would woo its wielder must be boldest of the bold.

Beneath its folds enormous three spans thick was the shield,
If all be true they tell us, that Brunhild bore in field.
Of steel and gold compacted all gorgeously it glow'd.
Four chamberlains, that bore it, stagger'd beneath the load.

Grimly smil'd Sir Hagan, Trony's champion strong,
And mutter'd, as he mark'd it trail'd heavily along,
"How now, my lord king Gunther? who thinks to scape with life?
This love of yours and lady—'faith she's the devil's wife."
. . . .
Then to the maid was carried heavily and slow
A strong well-sharpen'd jav'lin, which she ever us'd to throw,

Huge and of weight enormous, fit for so strong a queen,
Cutting deep and deadly with its edges keen.

To form the mighty spear-head a wondrous work was done;
Three weights of iron and better were welden into one;
The same three men of Brunhild's scarcely along could bring;
Whereat deeply ponder'd the stout Burgundian king.

To himself thus thought he, "What have I not to fear?
The devil himself could scarcely 'scape from such danger clear.
In sooth, if I were only in safety by the Rhine,
Long might remain this maiden free from all suit of mine."
. . . .

Stanza 464-483.
Then was the strength of Brunhild to each beholder shown.
Into the ring by th' effort of panting knights a stone
Was borne of weight enormous, massy and large and round.
It strain'd twelve brawny champions to heave it to the ground.

This would she cast at all times when she had hurl'd the

spear;
The sight the bold Burgundians fill'd with care and fear.
Quoth Hagan, "she's a darling to lie by Gunther's side.
Better the foul fiend take her to serve him as a bride."

    Her sleeve back turn'd the maiden, and bar'd her arm of snow,
Her heavy shield she handled, and brandished to and fro
High o'er her head the jav'lin; thus began the strife.
Bold as they were, the strangers each trembled for his life;

    And had not then to help him come Siegfried to his side,
At once by that grim maiden had good King Gunther died.
Unseen up went he to him, unseen he touch'd his hand.
His trains bewilder'd Gunther was slow to understand.

    "Who was it just now touch'd me?" thought he and star'd around
To see who could be near him; not a soul he found.
Said th' other, "I am Siegfried, thy trusty friend and true;
Be not in fear a moment for all the queen can do."

    Said he, "off with the buckler and give it me to bear;
Now, what I shall advise thee, mark with thy closest care.
Be it thine to make the gestures, and mine the work to do."

Glad man was then king Gunther, when he his helpmate knew.

"But all my trains keep secret; thus for us both 'twere best;
Else this o'erweening maiden, be sure, will never rest,
Till her grudge against thee to full effect she bring.
See where she stands to face thee so sternly in the ring!"

With all her strength the jav'lin the forceful maiden threw.
It came upon the buckler massy, broad, and new,
That in his hand unshaken, the son of Sieglind bore.
Sparks from the steel came streaming, as if the breeze before.

Right through the groaning buckler the spear tempestuous broke;
Fire from the mail-links sparkled beneath the thund'ring stroke,
Those two mighty champions stagger'd from side to side;
But for the wondrous cloud-cloak both on the spot had died.

From the mouth of Siegfried burst the gushing blood;
Soon he again sprung forward; straight snatch'd the hero

good
The spear that through his buckler she just had hurl'd amain,
And sent it at its mistress in thunder back again.

 Thought he "'t were sure a pity so fair a maid to slay;"
So he revers'd the jav'lin, and turn'd the point away.
Yet, with the butt end foremost, so forceful was the throw,
That the sore-smitten damsel totter'd to and fro.

 From her mail fire sparkled as driven before the blast;
With such huge strength the jav'lin by Sieglind's son was cast,
That 'gainst the furious impulse she could no longer stand.
A stroke so sturdy never could come from Gunther's hand.

 Up in a trice she started, and straight her silence broke,
"Noble knight, Sir Gunther, 'thank thee for the stroke."
She thought 't was Gunther's manhood had laid her on the lea;
No! It was not he had fell'd her, but a mightier far than he.

 Then turn'd aside the maiden; angry was her mood;
On high the stone she lifted rugged and round and rude,
And brandish'd it with fury, and far before her flung,
Then bounded quick behind it, that loud her armour rung.

Twelve fathoms' length or better the mighty mass was thrown,
But the maiden bounded further than the stone.
To where the stone was lying Siegfried fleetly flew
Gunther did but lift it, th' Unseen it was, who threw.

Bold, tall, and strong was Siegfried, the first all knights among;
He threw the stone far further, behind it further sprung.
His wondrous arts had made him so more than mortal strong,
That with him as he bounded, he bore the king along.

The leap was seen of all men, there lay as plain the stone,
But seen was no one near it, save Gunther all alone.
Brunhild was red with anger, quick came her panting breath;
Siegfried has rescued Gunther that day from certain death.

Then all aloud fair Brunhild bespake her courtier band,
Seeing in the ring at distance unharm'd her wooer stand,
"Hither, my men and kinsmen: low to my better bow;
I am no more your mistress; you're Gunther's liegemen now."

Down cast the noble warriors their weapons hastily,
And lowly kneel'd to Gunther the king of Burgundy.
To him as to their sovran was kingly homage done,
Whose manhood, as they fancied, the mighty match had won.

He fair the chiefs saluted bending with gracious look;
Then by the hand the maiden her conquering suitor took,
And granted him to govern the land with sovran sway;
Whereat the warlike nobles were joyous all and gay.

Upon the return to Worms the double marriage feast is celebrated—the weddings of Gunther and Brunhild, of Siegfried and Kriemhild. A second time is Gunther compelled to ask the help of Siegfried in conquering Brunhild, who again thinks that Gunther is the conqueror. From this second struggle Siegfried carries away Brunhild's ring and girdle, which he gives to Kriemhild. Siegfried and Kriemhild depart to his country, and not until after ten years do they visit again the court of Gunther. At the festival given in honor of this visit, the two queens, looking on at the knightly games, fall into a bitter quarrel concerning the prowess of their husbands. Kriemhild boasts to Brunhild that it was Siegfried and not Gunther who overcame her in both struggles. To prove her taunt she shows the girdle and ring. Brunhild is thrown into violent anger by the insult and desires only vengeance upon Siegfried and

Kriemhild. Hagen, the most valiant of Gunther's vassals, takes up her cause, and seeks opportunity to kill Siegfried. A war against the Saxons is declared, in which Siegfried offers to assist Gunther. On the eve of the departure to battle, Hagen visits Kriemhild. She begs him to protect Siegfried, and tells him the story of her husband's one vulnerable spot—when Siegfried had killed the dragon, he bathed in its blood, and was rendered invulnerable, except in one spot, where a lime leaf fell between his shoulders. This spot the dragon blood did not touch. Kriemhild promises to mark this spot with a silken cross, that Hagen may the better protect her husband. The next morning the excursion against the Saxons is withdrawn, and the heroes conclude to go on a hunting party.

THE HUNTING AND THE DEATH OF SIEGFRIED. Stanzas 944-958.

Gunther and Hagan, the warriors fierce and bold,
To execute their treason, resolved to scour the wold.
The bear, the boar, the wild bull, by hill or dale or fen,
To hunt with keen-edg'd javelins; what fitter sport for valiant
men?

In lordly pomp rode with them Siegfried the champion strong.
Good store of costly viands they brought with them along.
Anon by a cool runnel he lost his guiltless life.
'T was so devis'd by Brunhild, King Gunther's moody wife.

But first he sought the chamber where he his lady found.
He and his friends already had on the sumpters bound
Their gorgeous hunting raiment; they o'er the Rhine would go.
Never before was Kriemhild sunk so deep in woe.

On her mouth of roses he kiss'd his lady dear;
"God grant me, dame, returning in health to see thee here;
So may those eyes see me too; meanwhile be blithe and gay
Among thy gentle kinsmen; I must hence away."

Then thought she on the secret (the truth she durst not tell)
How she had told it Hagan; then the poor lady fell
To wailing and lamenting that ever she was born.
Then wept she without measure, sobbing and sorrow-worn.

She thus bespake her husband, "Give up that chace of thine.
I dreamt last night of evil, how two fierce forest swine
Over the heath pursued thee; the flowers turn'd bloody red.
I cannot help thus weeping; I'm chill'd with mortal dread.

I fear some secret treason, and cannot lose thee hence,

Lest malice should be borne thee from misconceiv'd offence.
Stay, my beloved Siegfried, take not my words amiss.
'T is the true love I bear thee that bids me counsel this."

"Back shall I be shortly, my own beloved mate.
Not a soul in Rhineland know I, who bears me hate.
I'm well with all thy kinsmen; they're all my firm allies;
Nor have I from any e'er deserv'd otherwise."

"Nay! do not, dearest Siegfried! 't is e'en thy death I dread.
Last night I dreamt, two mountains fell thundering on thy head,
And I no more beheld thee; if thou from me wilt go,
My heart will sure be breaking with bitterness of woe."

Round her peerless body his clasping arms he threw;
Lovingly he kiss'd her, that faithful wife and true;
Then took his leave, and parted;—in a moment all was o'er—
Living, alas poor lady! she saw him never more.

In the chase Siegfried prefers to hunt with a single limehound.
But he achieves most marvelous feats of skill and strength.

Stanzas 962-971.

All, that the limehound started, anon with mighty hand
Were slain by noble Siegfried the chief of Netherland.
No beast could there outrun him, so swift is steed could race;
He won from all high praises for mastery in the chace.

Whatever he attempted, he went the best before.
The first beast he encounter'd was a fierce half-bred boar.
Him with a mighty death-stroke he stretch'd upon the ground;
Just after in a thicket a lion huge he found.

Him the limehound started; his bow Sir Siegfried drew;
With a keen-headed arrow he shot the lion through.
But three faint bounds thereafter the dying monster made.
His wond'ring fellow-huntsmen thanks to Sir Siegfried paid.

Then one upon another a buffalo, an elk
He slew, four strong ureoxen, and last a savage shelk.
No beast, how swift soever, could leave his steed behind;
Scarcely their speed could profit the flying hart or hind
. . . .
They heard then all about them, throughout those forest grounds,
Such shouting and such baying of huntsmen and of hounds,

That hill and wood re-echoed with the wild uproar.
Th' attendants had uncoupled four and twenty dogs or more.

Then full many a monster was doom'd his last to groan.
They thought with glad expectance to challenge for their own
The praise for the best hunting; but lower sunk their pride,
When to the tryst-fire shortly they saw Sir Siegfried ride.

The hunting now was over for the most part at least;
Game was brought in plenty and skins of many a beast
To the place of meeting, and laid the hearth before.
Ah! to the busy kitchen what full supplies they bore!
. . . .

The chase being done, the hunters are summoned to a feast in a neighboring glade. Here, though they are served with a profusion of sumptuous viands, there is, according to Hagen's plot, no wine to drink. When, toward the end of the meal Siegfried is tormented with thirst, Hagen tells him of a cool runnel near by under a linden, and proposes that he and Gunther and Siegfried shall try a race to this brook. Siegfried gaily consents, and boasts that he will run with all his clothing and his weapons upon him.

Stanzas 1005-1029.
King Gunther and Sir Hagan to strip were nothing slow;

Both for the race stood ready in shirts as white as snow.
Long bounds, like two wild panthers o'er the grass they took,
But seen was noble Siegfried before them at the brook.

    Whate'er he did, the warrior high o'er his fellows soar'd.
Now laid he down his quiver, and quick ungirt his sword.
Against the spreading linden he lean'd his mighty spear.
So by the brook stood waiting the chief without a peer.

    In every lofty virtue none with Sir Siegfried vied.
Down he laid his buckler by the water's side.
For all the thirst that parch'd him, one drop he never drank
Till the king had finished; he had full evil thank.

    Cool was the little runnel, and sparkled clear as glass.
O'er the rill king Gunther knelt down upon the grass.
When he his draught had taken, he rose and stepp'd aside.
Full fain alike would Siegfried his thirst have satisfied.

    Dear paid he for his courtesy; his bow, his matchless blade,
His weapons all, Sir Hagan far from their lord convey'd,
Then back sprung to the linden to seize his ashen spear,
And to find out the token survey'd his vesture near;

Then, as to drink Sir Siegfried down kneeling there he found,
He pierc'd him through the croslet, that sudden from the wound
Forth the life-blood spouted e'en o'er his murderer's weed.
Never more will warrior dare so foul a deed.

Between his shoulders sticking he left the deadly spear.
Never before Sir Hagan so fled for ghastly fear,
As from the matchless champion whom he had butcher'd there.
Soon as was Sir Siegfried of the mortal wound aware,

Up he from the runnel started, as he were wood
Out from betwixt his shoulders his own hugh boar-spear stood.
He thought to find his quiver or his broadsword true.
The traitor for his treason had then receiv'd his due.

But, ah! the deadly-wounded nor sword nor quiver found;
His shield alone beside him lay there upon the ground.
This from the bank he lifted and straight at Hagan ran;
Him could not then by fleetness escape king Gunther's man.

E'en to the death though wounded, he hurl'd it with such power,
That the whirling buckler scatter'd wide a shower
Of the most precious jewels, then straight in shivers broke.
Full gladly had the warrior then vengeance with that stroke.

E'en as it was, his manhood fierce Hagan level'd low.
Loud, all around, the meadow rang with the wondrous blow.
Had he in hand good Balmung, the murderer he had slain.
His wound was sore upon him; he writh'd in mortal pain;

His lively colour faded; a cloud came o'er his sight:
He could stand no longer; melted all his might;
In his paling visage the mark of death he bore.
Soon many a lovely lady sorrow'd for him sore.

So the lord of Kriemhild among the flowerets fell.
From the wound fresh gushing his heart's blood fast did well.
Then thus amidst his tortures, e'en with his failing breath,
The false friends he upbraided who had contriv'd his death.

Thus spake the deadly-wounded, "Ay! cowards false as

hell!
To you I still was faithful; I serv'd you long and well;
But what boots all?—for guerdon treason and death I've won.
By your friends, vile traitors! foully have you done.

Whoever shall hereafter from your loins be born,
Shall take from such vile fathers a heritage of scorn.
On me you have wreak'd malice where gratitude was due.
With shame shall you be banish'd by all good knights and true."

Thither ran all the warriors where in his blood he lay.
To many of that party sure it was a joyless day.
Whoever were true and faithful, they sorrow'd for his fall.
So much the peerless champion had merited of all.

With them the false king Gunther bewept his timeless end.
Then spake the deadly-wounded; "little it boots your friend
Yourself to plot his murder, and then the deed deplore.
Such is a shameful sorrow; better at once it were o'er."

Then spake the low'ring Hagan, "I know not why you moan.
Our cares all and suspicions are now for ever flown.

Who now are left, against us who'll dare to make defence?
Well's me, for all this weeping, that I have rid him hence."

    "Small cause hast thou," said Siegfried, "to glory in my fate.
Had I ween'd thy friendship cloak'd such murderous hate,
From such as thou full lightly could I have kept my life.
Now grieve I but for Kriemhild, my dear, my widow'd wife.
. . . .
Then further spake the dying, and speaking sigh'd full deep,
"Oh king! if thou a promise with any one wilt keep,
Let me in this last moment thy grace and favour find
For my dear love and lady, the wife I leave behind.

    Remember, she's thy sister, yield her a sister's right,
Guard her with faith and honour, as thou'rt a king and knight.
My father and my followers for me they long must wait.
Comrade ne'er found from comrade so sorrowful a fate."

    In his mortal anguish he writh'd him to and fro,
And then said, deadly groaning, "this foul and murderous blow
Deep will ye rue hereafter; this for sure truth retain,
That in slaying Siegfried you yourselves have slain."

With blood were all bedabbled the flowerets of the field.
Some time with death he struggled, as though he scorn'd to yield
E'en to the foe, whose weapon strikes down the loftiest head.
At last prone in the meadow lay mighty Siegfried dead.

They carry the body of Siegfried back to Worms, and lay it at Kriemhild's door. Here she finding it next morning. She has it carried to the church and stands by it while the heroes come to view it, expecting to discover the murderer.

KRIEMHILD'S TEST.
Stanza 1071-1078.

And now the night was over; forth peep'd the morning fair;
Straight had the noble lady thence to the minster bear
The matchless champion Siegfried, her husband lov'd so dear.
All her friends close follow'd with many a sigh and tear.

When they the minster enter'd, how many a bell was rung!
How many a priest on all sides the mournful requiem sung!
Then thither with his meiny came Dancrat's haughty son,

And thither too grim Hagan; it had been better left undone.

    Then spoke the king, "dear sister, woe worth this loss of thine!
Alas that such misfortune has happ'd to me and mine!
For sure the death of Siegfried we ever both must rue."
"Nay", said the mournful lady, "so without cause you do,

    For if you really rued it, never had it been.
I know, you have your sister forgotten quite and clean,
So I and my beloved were parted as you see.
Good God! would he had granted the stroke had fall'n on me!"

    Firmly they made denial; Kriemhild at once replied,
"Whoe'er in this is guiltless, let him this proof abide.
In sight of all the people let him approach the bier,
And so to each beholder shall the plain truth appear."

    It is a mighty marvel, which oft e'en now we spy,
That when the blood-stain'd murderer comes to the murder'd nigh,
The wounds break out a-bleeding; then too the same befell,
And thus could each beholder the guilt of Hagan tell.

The wounds at once burst streaming fast as they did before;
Those, who then sorrow'd deeply, now yet lamented more.
Then outspake king Gunther, "I give you here to know,
He was slain by robbers; Hagan struck ne'er a blow."

"Ay! well know I those robbers," his widow'd sister said;
"By the hands of his true comrades may God revenge the dead!
False Gunther, and false Hagan! 't was you, your friend that slew."
Thereat the knights of Siegfried grip'd to their swords anew.

After the burial of Siegfried, Kriemhild decides to remain at the court of Gunther, in the care of her brothers. Thither is brought the enormous treasures of the Niebelungen, which Siegfried had won, and of which he had been the guardian, and which now fell to Kriemhild. The crafty Hagen gains possession of this horde, and conceals it by sinking it in the Rhine, hoping some day to recover and enjoy it. For thirteen years Kriemhild remains at the court of her brother, brooding over her wrongs and meditating revenge. The second part of the poem begins by telling how Etzel, king of the Huns, proposed for the hand of the widowed Kriemhild, and how she finally, hoping to use him in her plan of vengeance, consents to a marriage with him and goes away with him into his land. Here for many years she lives the beloved queen of the Huns. But her purpose of vengeance never falters, and at last she persuades Etzel to invite her brothers to his court on a visit. Against many forebodings and warnings they come, Hagen with them. After numerous interesting episodes upon the journey, they arrive at Etzell's court and are handsomely welcomed. But the inevitable quarrel soon breaks out and a desperate fight begins. After a most desperate and bloody struggle, Gunther, Hagen, and a few followers are shut up in a hall. To this Kriemhild sets fire.

THE BURNING OF THE HALL.
Stanza, 2186-2194.

With that, the wife of Etzel had set the hall on fire.
How sore then were they tortur'd in burning anguish dire!
At once, as the wind freshen'd, the house was in a glow.
Never, I ween, were mortals in such extremes of woe.

"We all are lost together," each to his neighbour cried,
"It had been far better we had in battle died.
Now God have mercy on us! woe for this fiery pain!
Ah! what a monstrous vengeance the bloody queen has ta'en!"

Then faintly said another, "needs must we here fall dead;
What boots us now the greeting, to us by Etzel sped?
Ah me! I'm so tormented by thirst from burning heat,

That in this horrid anguish my life must quickly fleet."

    Thereat outspake Sir Hagan, the noble knight and good,
"Let each, by thirst tormented, take here a draught of blood.
In such a heat, believe me, 't is better far than wine.
Nought's for the time so fitting; such counsel, friends, is mine."

    With that straight went a warrior, where a warm corpse he found.
On the dead down knelt he; his helmet he unbound;
Then greedily began he to drink the flowing blood.
However unaccustom'd, it seem'd him passing good.

    "Now God requite thee, Hagan," the weary warrior cried,
"For such refreshing beverage by your advice supplied.
It has been my lot but seldom to drink of better wine.
For life am I thy servant for this fair hint of thine."

    When th' others heard and witness'd with that delight he quaff'd,
Yet many more among them drank too the bloody draught.

It strung again their sinews, and failing strength renew'd.
This in her lover's person many a fair lady rued.

    Into the hall upon them the fire-flakes thickly fell;
These with their shields they warded warily and well.
With smoke and heat together they were tormented sore.
Never, I ween, good warriors such burning anguish bore.

    Through smoke and flame cried Hagan, "stand close against the
wall;
Let not the burning ashes on your helm-laces fall.
Into the blood yet deeper tread every fiery flake.
In sooth, this feast of Kriemhild's is ghastly merry-make."

    One by one the champions fall, until only Hagen and Gunther, exhausted with fighting, are left to contend with Dietrich, the most Valisntof Etzel's vassals. The conclusion of the poem tells of the fate of Hagen, Gunther, and Kriemhild.

    THE FALL OF THE NIEBELUNGEN.
Stanza 2428-2459.

    Well knew the noble Dietrich how fierce and fell a knight
Was standing now against him; so warily the fight
'Gainst those tempestuous swordstrokes wag'd the good

lord of
Bern.
The strength and skill of Hagan he had not now to learn.

He fear'd too, mighty Balmung as down it swept amain;
Yet at times Sir Dietrich with craft would strike again,
Till that to sink before him he brought his foeman strong;
A fearful wound, he gave him that was both deep and long.

Sir Dietrich then bethought him, "thou'rt faint and ill bestead
I should win little worship, were I to strike thee dead.
I'll make a different trial, if thou can'st now be won
By main force for a pris'ner." With wary heed 't was done.

Down he threw his buckler; wondrous was his might;
He his arms resistless threw round Trony's knight.
So was by his stronger the main of strength subdued.
Thereat the noble Gunther remain'd in mournful mood.

His vanquish'd foe Sir Dietrich bound in a mighty band,
And led him thence to Kriemhild, and gave into her hand
The best and boldest champion that broadsword ever bore.
She after all her anguish felt comfort all the more.

For joy the queen inclin'd her before the welcome guest;
"Sir knight I in mind and body heaven keep thee ever blest!
By thee all my long sorrows are shut up in delight.
Even if death prevent not, thy service I'll requite."

"Fair and noble Kriemhild," thus Sir Dietrich spake,
"Spare this captive warrior, who full amends will make
For all his past transgressions; him here in bonds you see;
Revenge not on the fetter'd th' offences of the free."

With that she had Sir Hagan to durance led away,
Where no one could behold him, where under lock he lay.
Meanwhile the fierce king Gunther shouted loud and strong,
"Whither is gone the Berner? he hath done me grievous wrong."

Straight, at the call, to meet him Sir Dietrich swiftly went.
Huge was the strength of Gunther, and deadly his intent.
There he no longer dallied; from th' hall he forward ran;
Sword clash'd with sword together, as man confronted man.

Howe'er renown'd was Dietrich, and train'd in combat well,
Yet Gunther fought against him so furious and so fell,
And bore him hate so deadly, now friendless left and lone,
It seemed past all conceiving, how Dietrich held his own.

Both were of mighty puissance, and neither yielded ground;
Palace and airy turret rung with their strokes around,
As their swift swords descending their temper'd helmets hew'd
Well there the proud king Gunther display'd his manly mood.

Yet him subdued the Berner, as Hagan erst befell;
Seen was the blood of the warrior forth through his mail to well
Beneath the fatal weapon that Dietrich bore in fright.
Tir'd as he was, still Gunther had kept him like a knight.

So now at length the champion was bound by Dietrich there,
How ill soe'er it fitteth a king such bonds to bear.
Gunther and his fierce liegeman if he had left unbound,
He ween'd they'd deal destruction on all, whome'er they found.

Then by the hand Sir Dietrich took the champion good.
And in his bonds thence led him to where fair Kriemhild stood.
She cried, "thou'rt welcome, Gunther, hero of Burgundy."
"Now God requite you, Kriemhild, if you speak lovingly."

Said he, "I much should thank you, and justly, sister dear,
If true affection prompted the greeting which I hear;
But, knowing your fierce temper, proud queen, too well I see,
Such greeting is a mocking of Hagan and of me."

Then said the noble Berner, "high-descended dame,
Ne'er have been brought to bondage knights of such peerless fame,
As those, whom you, fair lady, now from your servant take.
Grant these forlorn and friendless fair treatment for my sake."

She said she fain would do so; then from the captive pair
With weeping eyes Sir Dietrich retir'd and left them there.
Straight a bloody vengeance wreak'd Etzell's furious wife
On those redoubted champions, and both bereft of life.

In dark and dismal durance them kept apart the queen,
So that from that hour neither was by the other seen,
Till that at last to Hagan her brother's head she bore.
On both she took with vengeance as tongue ne'er told before.

To the cell of Hagan eagerly she went;
Thus the knight bespake she, ah! with what fell intent!
"Wilt thou but return me what thou from me hast ta'en,
Back thou may'st go living to Burgundy again."

Then spake grim-visag'd Hagan, "you throw away your prayer,
High-descended lady; I took an oath whilere,
That, while my lords were living, or of them only one,
I'd ne'er point out the treasure; thus 't will be given to none."

Well knew the subtle Hagan, she ne'er would let him 'scape.
Ah! when did ever falsehood assume so foul a shape?
He fear'd, that, soon as ever the queen his life had ta'en,
She then would send her brother to Rhineland back again.

"I'll make an end, and quickly," Kriemhild fiercely spake.

Her brother's life straight had she in his dungeon take.
Off his head was smitten; she bore it by the hair
To the lord of Trony; such sight he well could spare.

    A while in gloomy sorrow he view'd his master's head;
Then to remorseless Kriemhild thus the warrior said;
"E'en to thy wish this business thou to an end hast brought,
To such an end, moreover, as Hagan ever thought.

    Now the brave king Gunther of Burgundy is dead
Young Giselher and eke Gernot alike with him are sped;
So now, where lies the treasure, none knows save God and me,
And told shall it be never, be sure, she-fiend! to thee."

    Said she, "ill hast thou quitted a debt so deadly scor'd;
At least in my possession I'll keep my Siegfried's sword.
My lord and lover bore it, when last I saw him go.
For him woe wring my bosom, that pass'd all other woe."

    Forth from the sheath she drew it; that could not be prevent;
At once to slay the champion was Kriemhild's stern intent.
High with both hands she heav'd it, and off his head did smite.
That was seen of king Etzel; he shudder'd at the sight.

"Ah!" cried the prince impassion'd, "harrow and welaway!
That the hand of a woman the noblest knight should slay,
That e'er struck stroke in battle, or ever buckler bore!
Albeit I was his foeman, needs must I sorrow sore."

Then said the aged Hildebrand, "let not her boast of gain,
In that by her contrivance this noble chief was slain.
Though to sore strait he brought me, let ruin on me light,
But I will take full vengeance for Trony's murdered knight."

Hildebrand the aged fierce on Kriemhild sprung:
To the death he smote her as his sword he swung.
Sudden and remorseless he his wrath did wreak.
What could then avail her her fearful thrilling shriek?

There now the dreary corpses stretch'd all around were seen;
There lay, hewn in pieces, the fair and noble queen.
Sir Dietrich and king Etzel, their tears began to start;
For kinsmen and for vassals each sorrow'd in his heart.

The mighty and the noble there lay together dead;
For this had all the people dole and drearihead.
The feast of royal Etzel was thus shut up in woe.
Pain in the steps of Pleasure treads ever here below.

'Tis more than I can tell you what afterwards befell,
Save that there was weeping for friends belov'd so well;
Knights and squires, dames and damsels, were seen lamenting all,
So here I end my story. This is THE NIBELUNGERS' FALL.

— Tr. by Littsom.

ROMANCES.

As elsewhere in Europe, the twelfth and thirteenth centuries in Germany produced numberless romances. These may be classed under (1) Romances of Arthur, (2) Romances of the Holy Graal, (3) Romances of Antiquity, and (4) Romances of Love and Chivalry. The chief poets of romances were Hartmann von Aue, Gottfried von Strassburg, and Wolfram von Eschenbach. A good example of the romance of love is "Der Arme Heinrich of Hartmann von Aue". "Poor Henry", to quote Scherer, "is a kind of Job, a man of noble birth; rich, handsome, and beloved, who is suddenly visited by God with the terrible affliction of leprosy, and who can be cured only by the lifeblood of a young maiden who is willing to die for him. The daughter of a peasant, to whose house he has retired in his despair, resolves to sacrifice her life for him. Heinrich accepts her offer, and the knife to kill her is already whetted, when a better feeling arises in his breast, and he refuses to take upon himself the guilt of her death, resolving to resign himself to the will of God. This resignation saves him; he recovers and marries the maiden." Our extracts are from the first and last of the poem.

HENRY THE LEPER.

Ll. 1-131.—

Once on a time, rhymeth the rhyme,
In Swabia land once on a time,
There was a nobleman so journeying,
Unto whose nobleness everything
Of virtue and high-hearted excellence
Worthy his line and his high pretense
With plentiful measure was meted out:
The land rejoiced in him round about.
He was like a prince in his governing—
In his wealth he was like a king;
But most of all by the fame far-flown
Of his great knightliness was he known,
North and south, upon land and sea.
By his name he was Henry of the Lea.
All things whereby the truth grew dim
Were held as hateful foes with him:
By solemn oath was he bounden fast
To shun them while his life should last.
In honour all his days went by:
Therefore his soul might look up high
To honorable authority.

    A paragon of all graciousness,
A blossoming branch of youthfulness,
A looking-glass to the world around,
A stainless and priceless diamond,
Of gallant 'haviour a beautiful wreath,
A home when the tyrant menaceth,
A buckler to the breast of his friend,
And courteous without measure or end;
Whose deeds of arms 'twere long to tell;
Of precious wisdom a limpid well,
A singer of ladies every one,
And very lordly to look upon
In feature and hearing and countenance:
Say, failed he in anything, perchance,
The summit of all glory to gain.
And the lasting honour of all men.

    Alack! the soul that was up so high
Dropped down into pitiful misery;
The lofty courage was stricken low,
The steady triumph stumbled in woe,
And the world-joy was hidden in the dust,
Even as all such shall be and must.
He whose life in the senses centreth
Is already in the shades of death.
The joys, called great, of this under-state
Burn up the bosom early and late;
And their shining is altogether vain,
For it bringeth anguish and trouble and pain,
The torch that flames for men to see
And wasteth to ashes inwardly

Is verily but an imaging
Of man's own life, the piteous thing.
The whole is brittleness and mishap:
We sit and dally in Fortune's lap
Till tears break in our smiles betwixt,
And the shallow honey-draught be mix'd
With sorrow's wormwood fathom-deep.
Oh! rest not therefore, man, nor sleep:
In the blossoming of thy flower-crown
A sword is raised to smite thee down.

    It was thus with Earl Henry, upon whom for his pride God sent a leprosy, as He did upon Job. But he did not bear his affliction as did Job.

    Its duteousness his heart forgot;
His pride waxed hard, and kept its place,
But the glory departed from his face,
And that which was his strength, grew weak.
The hand that smote him on the cheek
Was all too heavy. It was night,
Now, and his sun withdrew its light.
To the pride of his uplifted thought
Much woe the weary knowledge brought
That the pleasant way his feet did wend
Was all passed o'er and had an end.
The day wherein his years had begun
Went in his mouth with a malison.
As the ill grew stronger and more strong,—
There was but hope bore him along;
Even yet to hope he was full fain

That gold might help him back again
Thither whence God had cast him out.
Ah! weak to strive and little stout
'Gainst Heaven the strength that he possessed.
North and south and east and west,
Far and wide from every side,
Mediciners well proved and tried
Came to him at the voice of his woe;
But, mused and pondered they ever so,
They could but say, for all their care,
That he must be content to bear
The burthen of the anger of God;
For him there was no other road.
Already was his heart nigh down
When yet to him one chance was shown;
For in Salerno dwelt, folk said,
A leach who still might lend him aid,
Albeit unto his body's cure,
All such had been as nought before.

Earl Henry visits the leach in Salerno whom he implores to tell him the means by which he may be healed.

Quoth the leach, "Then know them what they are;
Yet still all hope must stand afar.
Truly if the cure for your care
Might be gotten anyway anywhere,
Did it hide in the furthest parts of earth,
This-wise I had not sent you forth.
But all my knowledge hath none avail;
There is but one thing would not fail:

An innocent virgin for to find,
Chaste, and modest, and pure in mind,
Who to save you from death might choose
Her own young body's life to lose;
The heart's blood of the excellent maid—
That and nought else can be your aid.
But there is none will be won thereby
For the love of another's life to die.

    "'T was then poor Henry knew indeed
That from his ill he might not be freed,
Sith that no woman he might win
Of her own will to act herein.
Thus got he but an ill return
For the journey he made unto Salerne,
And the hope he had upon that day
Was snatched from him and rent away.
Homeward he hied him back: fall fain
With limbs in the dust he would have lain.
Of his substance—lands and riches both—
He rid himself; even as one doth
Who the breath of the last life of his hope
Once and forever hath rendered up.
To his friends he gave and to the poor,
Unto God praying evermore
The spirit that was in him to save,
And make his bed soft in the grave.
What still remained aside he set
For Holy Church's benefit.
Of all that heretofore was his
Nought held he for himself, I wis,

Save one small house with byre and field:
There from the world he lived concealed,—
There lived he, and awaited Death,
Who being awaited, lingereth.
Pity and ruth his troubles found
Alway through all the country round.
Who heard him named, had sorrow deep
And for his piteous sake would weep.

The poor man who tilled Earl Henry's field had a daughter, a sweet and tender maiden who, out of love for Henry and a heart of Christ-like pity, at last offers herself to die for him. After a struggle Henry accepts the sacrifice. But when he knows it is about to be made his heart rises against it and he refuses to permit it. At this the maiden is much grieved. She takes it as a token that she is not pure enough to be offered for him. She prays for a sign that she may hope to become wholly cleansed. In answer to this prayer Earl Henry is in one night cleansed of the leprosy. He then joyfully takes the maiden for his bride and leads her before his kinsman and nobles for their consent.

"Then," quoth the Earl, "hearken me this.
The damozel who standeth here,—
And whom I embrace, being most dear,—
She it is unto whom I owe
The grace it hath pleased God to bestow.
He saw the simple spirited
Earnestness of the holy maid,
And even in guerdon of her truth
Gave me back the joys of my youth,

Which seemed to be lost beyond all doubt,
And therefore I have chosen her out
To wed with me knowing her free.
I think that God will let this be.
Lo! I enjoin ye, with God's will
That this my longing ye fulfill.
I pray ye all have but one voice
And let your choice go with my choice."

    Then the cries ceased, and the counter-cries,
And all the battle of advice,
And every lord, being content
With Henry's choice, granted assent.

    Then the priests came to bind as one
Two lives in bridal unison,
Into his hand they folded hers,
Not to be loosed in coming years,
And uttered between man and wife
God's blessing on the road of this life.
Many a bright and pleasant day
The twain pursued their steadfast way,
Till hand in hand, at length they trod
Upward to the kingdom of God.
Even as it was with them, even thus,
And quickly, it must be with us.
To such reward as theirs was then,
God help us in His hour. Amen.

— Tr. by Rossetti.

THE MINNESINGERS.

In the twelfth century, Germany had a remarkable outburst of lyric poetry, chiefly songs of love. The influence of the crusades, the spread of the romances of Arthur and Charlemagne roused over all Germany the spirit of poetry. The poets of this new movement are called Minnesingers. It is interesting to notice that the same poets who wrote these love lyrics, wrote also long romances of chivalry; the greatest names among them being Hartmann von Aue, Wolfram von Eschenbach, Heinrich von Ofterdingen, Gottfried von Strassburg, and Walther von der Vogelweide. They were of all ranks, but chiefly belonged to the upper classes—knights, squires, princes, and even kings being numbered among them. Their extraordinarily large number may be gathered from the fact that from the twelfth century alone the names of one hundred and sixty Minnesingers have come down to us. Their names and their songs have been handed down largely by tradition, since the mass of them could neither read nor write, and for a century or more their work was preserved orally.

The subject of these songs was almost always love—generally love of a sweetheart; sometimes of the simpler aspects of nature, sometimes the love of the Virgin. Besides this they wrote also many didactic, religious, and patriotic songs. The rhythmical and metrical structure of their verse was very complicated and generally very skillful, sometimes, however, running into eccentricities and barren technicalities. The Minnesinger generally composed the music of his song at the same time with the verse.

The bloom of the Minnesong passed away in the latter half of the thirteenth century. The songs became theological, didactic, political, more and more forced and complicated in form, more and more filled with quaint new figures, far-fetched conceits, and obscure allusions. Then gradually developed the school of the Meistersingers, who formed themselves into a guild of poets to which only those were admitted who passed examination upon the difficult technical rules that had been built up. The poetry of the Meistersinigers was, for the most part, tedious and artificial. The poets were not nobles and soldiers, but burghers and artisans. They reached their highest development in the sixteenth century. The most famous of them was Hans Sachs (1494-1575), who, in the space of fifty-three years, wrote 6181 pieces of verse.

DIETMAR VON AIST. Twelfth Century.
By the heath stood a lady
All lonely and fair;
As she watched for her lover,
A falcon flew near.
"Happy falcon!" she cried
"Who can fly where he list,
And can choose in the forest
The tree he loves best!

"Thus, too, had I chosen
One knight for mine own,
Him my eye had selected,
Him prized I alone:
But other fair ladies

Have envied my joy,
And why? for I sought not
Their bliss to destroy.

 "As to thee, lovely summer,
Returns the birds' strain,
As on yonder green linden
The leaves spring again,
So constant doth grief
At my eyes overflow,
And wilt not thou, dearest,
Return to me now?"

 "Yes, come, my own hero,
All others desert!
When first my eye saw thee,
How graceful thou wert;
How fair was thy presence,
How graceful, how bright!
Then think of me only,
My own chosen knight!"
. . . . . .
There sat upon the linden-tree
A bird and sang its strain;
So sweet it sang, that, as I heard,
My heart went back again:
It went to one remembered spot,
I saw the rose-trees grow,
And thought again the thoughts of love

There cherished long ago.

  A thousand years to me it seems
Since by my fair I sat,
Yet thus to have been a stranger long
Was not my choice, but fate:
Since then I have not seen the flowers,
Nor heard the birds' sweet song;
My joys have all too briefly passed,
My griefs been all too long.

  — Tr. by Taylor.

  WALTHER VON DER VOGELWEIDE. Early nineteenth Century.
UNDER THE LINDEN.

  Under the linden
On the meadow
Where our bed arrange'd was,
There now you may find e'en
In the shadow Broken flowers and crushe'd grass.
Near the woods, down in the vale
Tandaradi!
Sweetly sang the nightingale.

  I, poor sorrowing one,
Came to the prairie,
Look, my lover had gone before.
There he received me—
Gracious Mary!—
That now with bliss I am brimming o'er.

Kissed he me? Ah, thousand hours!
Tandaradi!
See my mouth, how red it flowers!

    Then 'gan he making
Oh! so cheery,
From flowers a couch most rich outspread.
At which outbreaking
In laughter merry
You'll find, whoe'er the path does tread.
By the rose he can see
Tandaradi!
Where my head lay cozily.

    How he caressed me
Knew it one ever
God defend! ashamed I'd be.
Whereto he pressed me
No, no, never
Shall any know it but him and me
And a birdlet on the tree
Tandaradi!
Sure we can trust it, cannot we?

    — Tr. by Kroeger.

FROM THE CRUSADERS' HYMN.
Sweet love of Holy Spirit

Direct sick mind and steer it,
God, who the first didst rear it,
Protect thou Christendom.
It lies of pleasure barren
No rose blooms more in Sharon;
Comfort of all th' ill-starren,
Oh! help dispel the gloom!
Keep, Savior, from all ill us!
We long for the bounding billows,
Thy Spirit's love must thrill us,
Repentant hearts' true friend.
Thy blood for us thou'st given,
Unlocked the gates of heaven.
Now strive we as we've striven
To gain the blessed land.
Our wealth and blood grows thinner;
God yet will make us winner
Gainst him, who many a sinner
Holds pawne'd in his hand.
. . . .
God keep thy help us sending,
With thy right hand aid lending,
Protect us till the ending
When at last our soul us leaves,
From hell-fires, flaming clamor
Lest we fall 'neath the hammer!
Too oft we've heard with tremor,
How pitiably it grieves
The land so pure and holy
All helplessly and fearfully!
Jerusalem, weep lowly,
That thou forgotten art!
The heathen's boastful glory

Put thee in slavery hoary.
Christ, by thy name's proud story
In mercy take her part!
And help those sorely shaken
Who treaties them would maken
That we may not be taken
And conquered at the start.

— Tr. by Kroeger.

When from the sod the flowerets spring,
And smile to meet the sun's bright ray,
When birds their sweetest carols sing,
In all the morning pride of May,
What lovelier than the prospect there?
Can earth boast any thing more fair?
To me it seems an almost heaven,
So beauteous to my eyes that vision bright is given.

But when a lady chaste and fair,
Noble, and clad in rich attire,
Walks through the throng with gracious air,
As sun that bids the stars retire,
Then, where are all thy boastings, May?
What hast thou beautiful and gay,
Compared with that supreme delight?
We leave thy loveliest flowers, and watch that lady bright.

Wouldst thou believe me,—come and place
Before thee all this pride of May;

Then look but on my lady's face,
And which is best and brightest say:
For me, how soon (if choice were mine)
This would I take, and that resign,
And say, "Though sweet thy beauties, May,
I'd rather forfeit all than lose my lady gay!"

— Tr. by Taylor.

The Minnesingers wrote many songs in praise of the Virgin. She was the embodiment of pure womanhood, their constant object of devotion. The following extracts are taken from a hymn to the Virgin, formerly attributed to Gottfried von Strassburg. It is one of the greatest of the Minnesongs. It consists of ninety-three stanzas, of which six are given.

Stanza 1.—
Ye who your life would glorify
And float in bliss to God on high,
There to dwell nigh
His peace and love's salvation;
Who fain would learn how to enroll
All evil under your control,
And rid your soul
Of many a sore temptation;
Give heed unto this song of love,
And follow its sweet story.
Then will its passing sweetness prove
Unto your hearts a winge'd dove
And upward move
Your souls to bliss and glory.

Stanza 12.—
Ye fruitful heavens, from your ways
Bend down to hear the tuneful lays
I sing in praise
Of her, the sainted maiden,
Who unto us herself has shown
A modest life, a crown and throne;
Whose love has flown
O'er many a heart grief-laden.
Thou too, O Christ, thine ear incline
To this my adoration,
In honor of that mother thine
Who ever blest must stay and shine,
For she's the shrine
Of God's whole vast creation.

Stanza 19.—
Thou sheen of flowers through clover place,
Thou lignum aloe's blooming face,
Thou sea of grace,
Where man seeks blessed landing.
Thou roof of rapture high and blest,
Through which no rain has ever passed,
Thou goodly rest,
Whose end is without ending.
Thou to help-bearing strength a tower
Against all hostile evils.
Thou parriest many a stormy shower

Which o'er us cast in darkest hour,
The hell worm's power
And other ruthless devils.

    Stanza 20.—
Thou art a sun, a moon, a star,
'Tis thou can'st give all good and mar,
Yea, and debar
Our enemies' great cunning.
That power God to thee hath given
That living light, that light of heaven:
Hence see we even
Thy praise from all lips running.
Thou' st won the purest, noblest fame,
In all the earth's long story,
That e'er attached to worldly name;
It shineth brightly like a flame;
All hearts the same
Adore its lasting glory.

    Stanza 82.—
To worship, Lady, thee is bliss,
And fruitful hours ne'er pass amiss
To heart that is
So sweet a guest's host-mansion.
He who thee but invited hath
Into his heart's heart love with faith,
Must live and bathe
In endless bliss-expansion.

To worship thee stirs up in man
A love now tame, now passion.
To worship thee doth waken, then
Love e'en in those love ne'er could gain;
Thus now amain
Shines forth thy love's concession.

From praising Mary, the poet passes to praising Christ.

Stanza 59.—
Thou cool, thou cold, thou warmth, thou heat,
Thou rapture's circle's central seat,
Who does not meet
With thee stays dead in sadness;
Each day to him appears a year,
Seldom his thoughts wear green bloom's gear;
He doth appear
Forever without gladness.
Thou art most truly our heart's shine
Our sun wide joy-inspiring;
A sweet heart's love for all that pine,
For all the sad a joyful shrine,
A spring divine
For the thirsty and desiring.

— Tr. by Kroeger.

CHAPTER V. ITALIAN LITERATURE.

There was no folk poetry and no popular literature in Mediaeval Italy. There were two reasons for this: (1) Italian history, political and intellectual, attaches itself very closely to that of Rome. The traditions of classic learning never died out. Hence the Italian nation was always too learned, too literary to develop a folk literature. (2) Italy was for many centuries dominated by ecclesiastical influence, and the people's minds were full of matters of religious and scholastic philosophy, which excluded art.

The Italians translated and adapted some of the epics, romances, and tales of other countries, during the earlier years of the Middle Ages; but they were written in Latin, or in a kind of French. They produced none of their own. There was no literature written in Italian before the thirteenth century.

In the thirteenth century (1250) there came the first outburst of Italian literature—religious songs, love songs, dramas, and tales. In almost every part of Italy men began to write. But it was in Tuscany, in Florence, that the most remarkable literary development of this period appeared. It was of the nature chiefly of lyric and allegoric poetry.

The work of this group of Tuscan poets was really the beginning of Italian literary art. Yet it was a finished art product, not at all like the beginnings of poetry in other countries.

The group numbered a dozen poets of considerable power and skill. The greatest of them and the greatest of Italian poets was Dante Alighieri. In Italian mediaeval literature three names stand out far above all others. They are Dante, Petrarch, and Boccaccio. So completely do they overshadow their contemporaries, that in making our selection of Italian literature we shall confine ourselves entirely to these three.

Dante Alighieri was born at Florence, in May, 1266, and died at
Ravenna in September, 1321. He had an eventful and pathetic life.
He was much in public affairs. He was banished from his native
city in 1302, and died in exile. His literary work is represented
chiefly by the following titles: "Vita Nuova, The New Life"; "Convito, The Banquet"; "De Monarchia, A Treatise on Monarchy";
"De Vulgari Eloquio, A Treatise on the Vulgar Tongue"; and
"Divina Commedia", his masterpiece and the master-work of the
Middle Ages.

FROM THE VITA NUOVA.

The "Vita Nuova" is a work of Dante's youth, a record of his early life and love. The title may be translated either Early Life or The New Life. From the nature of the work we may infer that the latter translation conveys the poet's thought. It implies that after his first sight of Beatrice he began a new existence. He saw her first when he was nine years old. Nine years later she greeted him for the first time. Inspired by this greeting he began the "Vita Nuova". [1] It is written in prose interspersed with sonnets and canzoni. We select for reproduction some of the sonnets from Rossetti's translation.

[1] When Dante first saw Beatrice she was eight years old. From that hour he says he loved her. She was the inspiration of his early poem; and afterward, in the Divine Comedy, she became the embodiment of his conception of divine wisdom. She was married quite young to Simon di Bardi, a citizen of Florence. She died in 1290, when only twenty-four years old.

I. Sonnets telling to other ladies the praise of Beatrice.
Ladies that have intelligence in love
Of mine own lady I would speak with you;
Not that I hope to count her praises through,
But telling what I may to ease my mind.
And I declare that when I speak thereof
Love sheds such perfect sweetness over me
That if my courage failed not, certainly
To him my listeners must be all resign'd.
Wherefore I will not speak in such large kind
That mine own speech should foil me, which were base;
But only will discourse of her high grace
In these poor words, the best that I can find,

With you alone dear dames and damozels:
'Twere ill to speak thereof with any else.

. . . .

My lady is desired in the high Heaven;
WHEREFORE, it now behoveth me to tell, saying:
Let any maid that would be well
Esteemed, keep with her; for as she goes by,
Into foul hearts a deadly chill is driven
By Love, that makes ill thoughts to perish there;
While any who endures to gaze on her
Must either be ennobled, or else die.
When one deserving to be raised so high
Is found, It is then her power attains its proof,
Making his heart strong for his soul's behoof
With the full strength of meek humility.
Also this virtue owns she, by God's will:
Who speaks with her can never come to ill.

II. On the death of Beatrice.

When mine eyes had wept for some while until they were so weary with weeping that I could no longer through them give ease to my sorrow, I bethought me that a few mournful words might stand me instead of tears. And therefore I proposed to make a poem, that weeping I might speak therein of her for whom so much sorrow had destroyed my spirit; and I then began:

The eyes that weep for pity of the heart
Have wept so long that their grief languisheth,
And they have no more tears to weep withal:
And now if I would ease me of a part

Of what, little by little, leads to death,
It must be done by speech, or not at all,
And because often, thinking I recall
How it was pleasant ere she went afar,
To talk of her with you, kind damozels,
I talk with no one else,
But only with such hearts as women's are.
And I will say,—still sobbing as speech fails,—
That she hath gone to Heaven suddenly,
And hath left Love below, to mourn with me.

III.
"Dante once prepared to paint an angel."
. . . .
"You and I would rather see that angel
Painted by the tenderness of Dante,—
Would we not?—than read a fresh Inferno."

— Browning's "One Word More".

On that day which fulfilled the year since my lady had been made of the citizens of eternal life, remembering me of her as I sat alone, I betook myself to draw the resemblance of an angel upon certain tablets. And while I did thus, chancing to turn my head, I perceived that some were standing beside me to whom I should have given courteous welcome, and that they were observing what I did; also I learned afterwards that they had been there a while before I perceived them. Perceiving whom, I arose for salutation and said: "Another was with me."

Afterwards, when they had left me, I set myself again to mine occupation, to wit, to the drawing figures of angels; in doing which, I conceived to write of this matter in rhyme, as for her anniversary, and to address my rhymes unto those who had just left me. It was then that I wrote the sonnet which saith "That Lady":

That lady of all gentle memories
Had lighted on my soul; whose new abode
Lies now, as it was well ordained of God,
Among the poor in heart where Mary is.
Love, knowing that dear image to be his,
Woke up within the sick heart sorrow-bowed,
Unto the sighs which are its weary load,
Saying, "Go forth." And they went forth, I wis
Forth went they from my breast that throbbed and ached;
With such a pang as oftentimes will bathe
Mine eyes with tears when I am left alone.
And still those sighs which drew the heaviest breath
Came whispering thus: "O noble intellect!
It is a year to-day that thou art gone."

IV. The Close of the Vita Nuova.
Beyond the sphere which spreads to widest space
Now soars the sigh that my heart sends above;
A new perception born of grieving Love
Guideth it upward the untrodden ways.
When it hath reached unto the end and stays,
It sees a lady round whom splendors move
In homage; till, by the great light thereof
Abashed, the pilgrim spirit stands at gaze.

It sees her such, that when it tells me this
Which it hath seen, I understand it not;
It hath a speech so subtle and so fine
And yet I know its voice within my thought
Often remembereth me of Beatrice:
So that I understand it, ladies mine.

After writing this sonnet, it was given unto me to behold a very wonderful vision,[1] wherein I saw things which determined me that I would say nothing further of this most blessed one, until such time as I could discourse more worthily of her. And to this end I labor all I can; as she well knoweth. Wherefore if it be His pleasure through whom is the life of all things, that my life continue with me a few years, it is my hope that I shall yet write concerning her what hath not before been written of any woman. After the which may it seem good unto Him who is the Master of Grace, that my spirit should go hence to behold the glory of its lady: to wit, the blessed Beatrice, who now gazeth continually on His countenance qui est per omnia soecula benedictus. Laus Deo.[2]

[1] This we may believe to be the vision of Hell, Purgatory, and Paradise, the vision which gave him the argument of the Divine Comedy.

[2] Who is blessed throughout all ages. Praise to God.

FROM THE DIVINE COMEDY.[1]

[1] Dante called his poem a comedy, he says, for two reasons: because it has a sad beginning and a cheerful ending, and because it is written in a "middle" style, treating alike of lowly and lofty things. Midway in life the poet

finds himself lost in the forest of worldly cares, beset by the three beasts, Pride, Avarice, and Worldly Pleasure. Virgil, who is the embodiment of moral philosophy, appears and leads him through the Hell of worldly sin and suffering, through the Purgatory of repentance, to the calm of the earthly Paradise. Mere philosophy can go no further. The poet is here taken under the guidance of Beatrice, the embodiment of divine wisdom, who leads him through Paradise to the throne of God. Such, in the briefest form, is the argument of the Divine Comedy; this statement carries the actual story and the allegory side by side. The first division of the triple vision is the Inferno. Dante's Inferno is an inverted cone, having its mouth in a deep rugged valley, its sides sloping down to the center of the earth. When Lucifer fell from heaven the earth retired before him, making this hollow cone. This is divided into nine circles, in which the lost souls suffer. These souls are grouped into three main classes: the incontinent, the violent, and the fraudulent. The first circle of the Inferno is Limbo, where are the souls of children and the unbaptized; of the heathen philosophers and poets. They are neither in pain nor glory, they do not shriek nor groan but only sigh.

I. The Poets in Limbo.—From the Inferno.
Broke the deep slumber in my brain a crash
Of heavy thunder, that I shook myself,
As one by main force roused. Risen upright,
My rested eyes I moved around, and search'd,
With fixed ken, to know what place it was
Wherein I stood. For certain, on the brink
I found me of the lamentable vale,
The dread abyss, that joins a thundrous sound
Of plaints innumerable. Dark and deep,

And thick with clouds o'erspread, mine eye in vain
Explored its bottom, nor could aught discern.
"Now let us to the blind world there beneath
Descend;" the bard began, all pale of look:
"I go the first, and thou shalt follow next."
Then I his alter'd hue perceiving, thus:
"How may I speed, if thou yieldest to dread,
Who still art wont to comfort me in doubt?"
He then: "The anguish of that race below
With pity stains my cheek, which thou for fear
Mistakest. Let us on. Our length of way
Urges to haste." Onward, this said, he moved;
And entering led me with him, on the bounds
Of the first circle that surrounds the abyss.

. . . .

We were not far
On this side from the summit, when I kenn'd
A flame, that o'er the darken'd hemisphere
Prevailing shined. Yet we a little space
Were distant, not so far but I in part
Discover'd that a tribe in honour high
That place possess'd. "O thou, who every art
And science valuest I who are these that boast
Such honour, separate from all the rest?"
He answer'd: "The renown of their great names,
That echoes through your world above, acquires
Favour in heaven, which holds them thus advanced."
Meantime a voice I heard: "Honour the bard
Sublime![1] his shade returns, that left us late!

No sooner ceased the sound, than I beheld

Four mighty spirits toward us bend their steps,
Of semblance neither sorrowful nor glad.
When thus my master kind began: "Mark him,
Who in his right hand bears that falchion keen,
The other three preceding, as their lord.
This is that Homer, of all bards supreme:
Flaccus the next, in satire's vein excelling;
The third is Naso; Lucan is the last.
Because they all that appellation own,
With which the voice singly accosted me,
Honouring they greet me thus, and well they judge."
So I beheld united the bright school
Of him the monarch of sublimest song,[2]

That o'er the others like an eagle soars.
When they together short discourse had held,
They turned to me, with salutation kind
Beckoning me; at the which my master smiled
Nor was this all; but greater honour still
They gave me, for they made me of their tribe;
And I was sixth amid so learn'd a band.

[1] The bard sublime—Virgil.

[2] The monarch of sublimest song—Homer.

II. Francesca da Rimini.[1]

[1] Francesca da Polenta was given in marriage by her father to Lanclotto da Rimini, a man brave, but of deformed person. His brother Paolo, who was exceedingly

handsome, won her affections. They were both put to death by Lagnciotto.

    From the Inferno. From Limbo the poet descends into the second circle, where the sin of lust is punished. The souls in this circle are driven forever round in a tyrannous gust of wind. They see Cleopatra and Helen and Paris and Tristan and many others whom Virgil names to the poet. Finally he sees two spirits approaching, whom he asks permission to address. To these he spoke:
"O wearied spirits! come, and hold discourse
With us, if by none else restrain'd." As doves
By fond desire invited, on wide wings
And firm, to their sweet nest returning home,
Cleave the air, wafted by their will along;
Thus issued, from that troop where Dido ranks,
They, through the ill air speeding—with such force
My cry prevail'd, by strong affection urged.
"O gracious creature and benign! who go'st
Visiting, through this element obscure,
Us, who the world with bloody stain imbrued;
If, for a friend, the King of all, we own'd,
Our prayer to him should for thy peace arise,
Since thou hast pity on our evil plight.
Of whatsoe'er to hear or to discourse
It pleases thee, that will we hear, of that
Freely with thee discourse, while e'er the wind,
As now, is mute. The land[1] that gave me birth,
Is situate on the coast, where Po descends
To rest in ocean with his sequent streams.
"Love, that in gentle heart is quickly learnt,
Entangled him by that fair form, from me
Ta'en in such cruel sort, as grieves me still!

Love, that denial takes from none beloved,
Caught me with pleasing him so passing well,
That, as thou seest' he yet deserts me not.
Love brought us to one death: Caina[2] waits
The soul, who split our life."
Such were their words;
At hearing which, downward I bent my looks,
And held them there so long, that the bard cried:
"What art thou pondering?" I in answer thus:
"Alas I by what sweet thoughts, what fond desire
Must they at length to that ill pass have reach'd!"
Then turning, I to them my speech addressed,
And thus began: "Francesca! your sad fate
Even to tears my grief and pity moves.
But tell me; in the time of your sweet sighs,
By what, and how Love granted, that ye knew
Your yet uncertain wishes?" She replied:
"No greater grief than to remember days
Of joy, when misery is at hand. That kens
Thy learn'd instructor. Yet so eagerly
If thou art bent to know the primal root,
From whence our love gat being, I will do
As one, who weeps and tells his tale. One day,
For our delight we read of Lancelot,[3]
How him love thrall'd. Alone we were, and no
Suspicion near us. Oft-times by that reading
Our eyes were drawn together, and the hue
Fled from our alter'd cheek. But at one point
Alone we fell. When of that smile we read,
The wished smile so rapturously kiss'd
By one so deep in love, then he, who ne'er
From me shall separate, at once my lips
All trembling kiss'd. The book and writer both

Were love's purveyors. In its leaves that day
We read no more." While thus one spirit spake,
The other wailed so sorely, that heart-struck
I, through compassion fainting, seem'd not far
From death, and like a corse fell to the ground.

[1] The land that gave me birth—Ravenna.

[2] Caina, the place to which murderers are doomed.

[3] Lancelot, one of the knights of the Round Table, the lover of Queen Guinevere.

III. Farinata.—From the Inferno.

The poet and his guide descend through the third circle where the sin of gluttony is punished; through the fourth, where they find the prodigal and avaricious; through the fifth where immersed in a filthy pool are the souls of the irascible. The sixth circle is the city of Dis, with walls of heated iron, filled within with open fiery tombs from which issue the groans of the heretics who are punished here. With two of these, Farinata degli Uberti[1] and Cavaleante Cavaleanti,[2] Dante holds converse.

[1] Farinata degli Uberti, a Florentine of great military ability, a leader of the Ghibelline, or imperial, party.

[2] Cavaleante Cavaleanti, a Florentine, of the Guelph, or Papal, party.

Now by a secret pathway we proceed,
Between the walls that hem the region round,
And the tormented souls: my master first,

I close behind his steps. "Virtue supreme!"
I thus began: "who through these ample orbs
In circuit lead'st me, even as thou will'st;
Speak thou, and satisfy my wish. May those,
Who lie within these sepulchres, be seen?
Already all the lids are raised, and none
O'er them keeps watch." He thus in answer spake:
"They shall be closed all, what-time they here
From Josaphat[1] return'd shall come, and bring
Their bodies, which above they now have left.
The cemetery on this part obtain,
With Epicurus, all his followers,
Who with the body make the spirit die.
Here therefore satisfaction shall be soon,
Both to the question ask'd, and to the wish [2]
Which thou conceal'st in silence." I replied:
"I keep not, guide beloved I from thee my heart
Secreted, but to shun vain length of words;
A lesson erewhile taught me by thyself."
"O Tuscan! thou, who through the city of fire
Alive art passing, so discreet of speech:
Here, please thee, stay awhile. Thy utterance
Declares the place of thy nativity
To be that noble land, with which perchance
I too severely dealt." Sudden that sound
Forth issued from a vault, whereat, in fear,
I somewhat closer to my leader's side
Approaching, he thus spake: "What dost thou? Turn: Lo!
Farinata, there, who hath himself
Uplifted: from his girdle upwards, all
Exposed, behold him." On his face was mine
Already fix'd: his breast and forehead there
Erecting, seem'd as in high scorn he held

E'en hell. Between the sepulchres, to him
My guide thrust me, with fearless hands and prompt;
This warning added: "See thy words be clear."
He, soon as there I stood at the tomb's foot,
Eyed me a space; then in disdainful mood
Address'd me: "Say what ancestors were thine."
I, willing to obey him, straight reveal'd
The whole, nor kept back aught: whence he, his brow
Somewhat uplifting, cried: "Fiercely were they
Adverse to me, my party, and the blood
From whence I sprang: twice, therefore, I abroad
Scatter'd them." "Though driven out, yet they each time
From all parts," answer'd I, "return'd; an art
Which yours have shown they are not skill'd to learn."
Then, peering forth from the unclosed jaw,
Rose from his side a shade,[3] high as the chin,
Leaning, methought, upon its knees upraised.
It look'd around, as eager to explore
If there were other with me; but perceiving
That fond imagination quench'd, with tears
Thus spake: "If thou through this blind prison go'st,
Led by thy lofty genius and profound,
Where is my son? and wherefore not with thee?
I straight replied: "Not of myself I come;
By him, who there expects me, through this clime
Conducted, whom perchance Guido thy son
Had in contempt."[4] Already had his words
And mode of punishment read me his name,
Whence I so fully answer'd. He at once
Exclaim'd' up starting, "How! said'st thou' he HAD?
No longer lives he? Strikes not on his eye
The blessed daylight?" Then, of some delay

I made ere my reply, aware, down fell
Supine, nor after forth appear'd he more.

[1] It was a common opinion that the general judgment would be held in the valley of Josaphat, or Jehoshaphat. Joel iii., 2.

[2] The wish-Dante's wish was to speak with the followers of Epicurus, of whom were Farinata and Cavalcante.

[3] A shade—Cavalcante.

[4] Guido, thy son had in contempt—Guido the son of Cavalcante Cavalcanti, a Tuscan poet, the friend of Dante. But being fonder of philosophy than of poetry was perhaps not an admirer of Virgil.

V. The Hypocrites. From the Inferno.

In the seventh circle, which is divided into three rounds, or gironi, the violent are tormented. The eighth circle is divided into ten concentric fosses, or gulfs, in each of which some variety of fraudulent sinners is punished. In the sixth gulf are the hypocrites.

There in the depth we saw a painted tribe,
Who paced with tardy steps around, and wept,
Faint in appearance and o'ercome with toil.
Caps had they on, with hoods, that fell low down
Before their eyes, in fashion like to those
Worn by the monks in Cologne.[1]
Their outside Was overlaid with gold, dazzling to view,
But leaden all within, and of such weight,
That Frederick's [2] compared to these were straw.
Oh, everlasting wearisome attire!
We yet once more with them together turn'd

To leftward, on their dismal moan intent.
But by the weight opprest, so slowly came
The fainting people, that our company
Was changed, at every movement of the step.
I staid, and saw two spirits in whose look
Impatient eagerness of mind was mark'd
To overtake me; but the load they bare
And narrow path retarded their approach.
Soon as arrived, they with an eye askance
Perused me, but spake not: then turning, each
To other thus conferring said: "This one
Seems, by the action of his throat, alive;
And, be they dead, what privilege allows
They walk unmantled by the cumbrous stole?"
Then thus to me: "Tuscan, who visitest
The college of the mourning hypocrites,
Disdain not to instruct us who thou art."
"By Arno's pleasant stream," I thus replied,
In the great city I was bred and grew,
And wear the body I have ever worn.
But who are ye, from whom such mighty grief,
As now I witness, courseth down your cheeks?
What torment breaks forth in this bitter woe?"
"Our bonnets gleaming bright with orange hue,"
One of them answer'd' "are so leaden gross,
That with their weight they make the balances
To crack beneath them. Joyous friars[3] we were,
Bologna's natives; Catalano I,
He Loderingo named; and by thy land
Together taken, as men use to take
A single and indifferent arbiter,
To reconcile their strifes. How there we sped,

Gardingo's vicinage [4] can best declare."
"O friars!" I began, "your miseries—"
But there brake off, for one had caught mine eye,
Fix'd to a cross with three stakes on the ground:
He, when he saw me, writhed himself, throughout
Distorted, ruffling with deep sighs his beard.
And Catalano, who thereof was 'ware,
Thus spake: "That pierced spirit,[5] whom intent
Thou view'st, was he who gave the Pharisees
Counsel, that it were fitting for one man
To suffer for the people. He doth lie
Transverse; nor any passes, but him first
Behoves make feeling trial how each weighs.
In straits like this along the foss are placed
The father of his consort,[6] and the rest
Partakers in that council, seed of ill
And sorrow to the Jews."

[1] The monks in Cologne. These monks wore their cowls unusually large.

[2] Frederick's. Frederick II. punished those guilty of high treason by wrapping them up in lead, and casting them into a furnace.

[3] Joyous friars. An order of knights (Frail Godenti) on two of whom the Ghibelline party at one time conferred the chief power of Florence. One was Catalano de' Malavolti, the other Loderingo di Liandolo. Their administration was unjust.

[4] Gardingo's vicinage. That part of the city inhabited

by the Ghibelline family of the Uberti, and destroyed, under the iniquitous administration of Catalano and Loderingo.

[5] That pierced spirit. Caiaphas.

[6] The father of his consort. Annas.

When the poets reach the ninth and last circle they see the souls of traitors lying in a frozen lake and in the midst Lucifer, the fallen archangel, in the very center of the earth. They slide down his icy sides, and begin to ascend to the earth's surface through a cavern "and thence come forth to see the stars again."

The second part of the Divine Comedy is the vision of Purgatory. When the solid earth retired before the falling Lucifer, making the hollow cone of hell, it was pushed out on the other side of the globe, forming the mountain of Purgatory. This is also divided into nine circles. In the first two are the souls of those who delayed repentance until death. In the other seven, the seven deadly sins are purged away. On the summit is the earthly paradise.

I. The Celestial Pilot.—From the Pargatorio.

The mountain of Purgatory is situated upon an island. While Virgil and Dante are standing looking across the water, they behold a boat laden with spirits for Purgatory under the guidance of an angel.

Meanwhile we linger'd by the water's brink,
Like men' who' musing on their road, in thought
Journey, while motionless the body rests.
When lo! as, near upon the hour of dawn,
Through the thick vapours
Mars with fiery beam

Glares down in west, over the ocean floor;
So seem'd, what once again I hope to view,
A light, so swiftly coming through the sea,
No winged course night equal its career.
From which when for a space I had withdrawn
Mine eyes, to make inquiry of my guide,
Again I look'd, and saw it grown in size
And brightness: then on either side appear'd
Something but what I knew not, of bright hue,
And by degrees from underneath it came
Another. My preceptor silent yet
Stood, while the brightness, that we first discern'd,
Open'd the form of wings: then when he knew
The pilot, cried aloud, "Down, down; bend low
Thy knees; behold God's angel: fold thy hands:
Now shalt thou see true ministers indeed.
Lo! how all human means he sets at nought;
So that nor oar he needs, nor other sail
Except his wings, between such distant shores.
Lo! how straight up to heaven he holds them rear'd,
Winnowing the air with those eternal plumes,
That not like mortal hairs fall off or change."
As more and more toward us came, more bright
Appear'd the bird of God, nor could the eye
Endure his splendour near: I mine bent down.
He drove ashore in a small bark so swift
And light, that in its course no wave it drank.
The heavenly steersman at the prow was seen,
Visibly written Blessed in his looks.
Within, a hundred spirits and more there sat.
"In Exitu [1] Israel de Egypto,"
All with one voice together sang, with what

In the remainder of that hymn is writ.
Then soon as with the sign of holy cross
He bless'd them, they at once leap'd out on land:
He, swiftly as he came, return'd.

[1] In Exitu Israel de Egypto—When Israel came out of Egypt.—Ps cxiv.

II. The Meeting with Sordello.—From the Purgatorio.

In the second circle of the mountain of Purgatory, Virgil and Dante encounter the spirit of Sordello,[1] detained among those who delayed repentance until death.

[1] Sordello. A Provencal soldier and poet, whose life is wrapt in romantic mystery. See Browning's poem "Sardello".

"But lo! a spirit there
Stands solitary' and toward us looks:
It will instruct us in the speediest way."
We soon approach'd it.
When my courteous guide began,
"Mantua," the shadow, in itself absorb'd,
Rose towards us from the place in which it stood,
And cried, "Mantuan! I am thy countryman, Sordello."
Each the other then embraced.
. . . .
After their courteous greetings joyfully
Seven times exchanged, Sordello backward drew
Exclaiming, "Who are ye?"—"Before this mount
By spirits worthy of ascent to God
Was sought, my bones had by Octavius care

Been buried. I am Virgil; for no sin
Deprived of heaven, except for lack of faith."
So answer'd him in few my gentle guide.

. . . .

"Glory of Latium!" he exclaim'd,
"In whom our tongue its utmost power display'd;
Boast of my honour'd birth-place I what desert
Of mine, what favour, rather, undeserved,
Shows thee to me? If I to hear that voice
Am worthy, say if from below thou comest,
And from what cloister's pale."—"Through every orb
Of that sad region," he replied, "thus far
Am I arrived, by heavenly influence led:
And with such aid I come. Not for my doing,
But for not doing, have I lost the sight
Of that high Sun, whom thou desirest, and who
By me too late was known. There is a place[1]
There underneath, not made by torments sad,
But by dun shades alone; where mourning's voice
Sounds not of anguish sharp, but breathes in sighs.
There I with little innocents abide,
Who by death's fangs were bitten, ere exempt
From human taint. There I with those abide,
Who the three holy virtues put not on,
But understood the rest, and without blame
Follow'd them all. But if thou know'st and canst,
Direct us how we soonest may arrive,
Where Purgatory its true beginning takes."
He answer'd thus: "We have no certain place
Assign'd us: upwards I may go, or round.
Far as I can, I join thee for thy guide.
But thou beholdest now how day declines;
And upwards to proceed by night, our power

Excels: therefore it may be well to choose
A place of pleasant sojourn. To the right
Some spirits sit apart retired. If thou
Consentest, I to these will lead thy steps:
And thou wilt know them, not without delight."

[1] A place there underneath. Limbo. See first selection from the Divine Comedy.

III. The Angel of the Gate.—From the Purgatorio.
The poets spend the night in this valley with Sordello and other spirits. In the morning they ascend to the gates of the real Purgatory. These are kept by an angel deputed by St. Peter.

Ashes, or earth taken dry out of the ground,
Were of one colour with the robe he wore.
From underneath that vestment forth he drew
Two keys, of metal twain: the one was gold,
Its fellow silver. With the pallid first,
And next the burnish'd, he so ply'd the gate,
As to content me well. "Whenever one
Faileth of these, that in the key-hole straight
It turn not, to this alley then expect
Access in vain." Such were the words he spake.
"One is more precious[1]: but the other needs,
Skill and sagacity, large share of each,
Ere its good task to disengage the knot
Be worthily perform'd.
From Peter these I hold, of him instructed that I err
Rather in opening, than in keeping fast;
So but the suppliant at my feet implore."
Then of that hallow'd gate he thrust the door,

Exclaiming, "Enter, but this warning hear:
He forth again departs who looks behind."
As in the hinges of that sacred ward
The swivels turn'd sonorous metal strong,
Harsh was the grating, nor so surlily
Roar'd the Tarpeian, when by force bereft Of good
Metellus, thenceforth from his loss
To leanness doom'd. Attentively I turn'd,
Listening the thunder that first issued forth;
And "We praise thee, O God," methought I heard,
In accents blended with sweet melody,
The strains came o'er mine ear, e'en as the sound
Of choral voices, that in solemn chant
With organ mingle, and, now high and clear
Come swelling, now float indistinct away.

[1] One is more precious. The golden key is the divine authority by which the priest gives absolution. The silver stands for the learning and wisdom necessary for the priest.

IV. Beatrice Appears to Dante and Rebukes Him. From the
Purgatorio.

Inside the gates of Purgatory rise seven successive circles, in which the seven deadly sins are purged; in the first, the sin of pride; in the second, that of envy; in the third, anger; in the fourth, lukewarmness; in the fifth, avarice; in the sixth, gluttony; in the seventh, incontinence is purged by fire. Having passed through all these, Dante and his guide ascend to the summit of the mountain, the earthly Paradise. Here Virgil ceases to guide the poet, but leaves him to choose for a while his own way. To him here descends Beatrice who, before assuming his further guidance, rebukes him for his manner of life on earth.

    At the last audit, so
The blest shall rise, from forth his cavern each
Uplifting lightly his new-vested flesh;
As, on the sacred litter, at the voice
Authoritative of that elder, sprang
A hundred ministers and messengers
Of life eternal. "Blessed thou, who comest!"
And, "Oh!" they cried, "from full hands scatter ye
Unwithering lilies": and, so saying, cast
Flowers over head and round them on all sides.
I have beheld, ere now, at break of day,
The eastern clime all roseate; and the sky
Opposed, one deep and beautiful serene;
And the sun's face so shaded, and with mists
Attemper'd, at his rising, that the eye
Long while endured the sight: thus, in a cloud
Of flowers, that from those hands angelic rose,
And down within and outside of the car
Fell showering, in white veil with olive wreathed,
A virgin in my view appear'd, beneath
Green mantle, robed in hue of living flame:
And o'er my spirit, that so long a time
Had from her presence felt no shuddering dread,
Albeit mine eyes discern'd her not, there moved
A hidden virtue from her, at whose touch
The power of ancient love was strong within me.
. . . .

Upon the chariot's same edge still she stood,
Immovable; and thus address'd her words:
"I shape mine answer, for his ear intended,
Who there stands weeping;[1] that the sorrow now
May equal the transgression. Not alone
Through operation of the mighty orbs,
That mark each seed to some predestined aim,
As with aspect or fortunate or ill
The constellations meet; but through benign
Largess of heavenly graces, which rain down
From such a height as mocks our vision, this man
Was, in the freshness of his being, such,
So gifted virtually, that in him
All better habits wonderously had thrived
He more of kindly strength is in the soil,
So much doth evil seed and lack of culture
Mar it the more, and make it run to wildness.
These looks sometime upheld him; for I showed
My youthful eyes, and led him by their light
In upright walking. Soon as I had reach'd
The threshold of my second age, and changed
My mortal for immortal; then he left me,
And gave himself to others. When from flesh
To spirit I had risen, and increase
Of beauty and of virtue circled me,
I was less dear to him, and valued less.
His steps were turn'd into deceitful ways,
Following false images of good, that make
No promise perfect. Nor availed me aught
To sue for inspirations, with the which,
I, both in dreams of night, and otherwise,
Did call him back; of them, so little reck'd him.
Such depth he fell, that all device was short

Of his preserving, save that he should view
The children of perdition. To this end
I visited the purlieus of the dead:
And one, who hath conducted him thus high,
Received my supplications urged with weeping.
It were a breaking of God's high decree,
If Lethe should be past, and such food[3] tasted,
Without the cost of some repentant tear."

[1] Who there stands weeping. Dante.

[2] Such food. The oblivion of sins.

The third part of the Divine Comedy is the vision of Paradise. Dante's Paradise is divided into ten heavens, or spheres. Through these in succession the poet is conducted by Beatrice, until in the tenth heaven, or the Empyrean, he comes into the visible presence of God.

I. The Visible Presence. From the Paradiso.
O eternal beam!
(Whose height what reach of mortal thought may soar?)
Yield me again some little particle
Of what thou then appearedst; give my tongue
Power' but to leave one sparkle of thy glory,
Unto the race to come' that shall not lose
Thy triumph wholly, if thou waken aught
Of memory in me, and endure to hear
The record sound in this unequal strain.
. . . .
O grace, unenvying of thy boon! that gavest
Boldness to fix so earnestly my ken
On the everlasting splendour, that I look'd,

While sight was unconsumed; and, in that depth,
Saw in one volume clasp'd of love, whate'er
The universe unfolds; all properties
Of substance and of accident, beheld,
Compounded, yet one individual light
The whole.

. . . .

In that abyss
Of radiance, clear and lofty, seem'd, methought,
Three orbs of triple hue,[1] clipt in one bound:
And, from another, one reflected seem'd,
As rainbow is from rainbow: and the third
Seem'd fire, breathed equally from both.
O speech! How feeble and how faint art thou, to give
Conception birth. Yet this to what I saw
Is less than little.
O eternal light!
Sole in thyself that dwell'st; and of thyself
Sole understood' past' present, or to come;
Thou smile'st, on that circling, which in thee
Seem'd as reflected splendour, while I mused;
For I therein, methought, in its own hue
Beheld our image painted: stedfastly
I therefore pored upon the view. As one,
Who versed in geometric lore, would fain
Measure the circle; and, though pondering long
And deeply, that beginning, which he needs,
Finds not: e'en such was I, intent to scan
The novel wonder, and trace out the form,
How to the circle fitted, and therein
How placed: but the flight was not for my wing:
Had not a flash darted athwart my mind,
And, in the spleen, unfolded what is sought.

Here vigour fail'd the towering fantasy:
But yet the will roll'd onward, like a wheel
In even motion' by the love impell'd,
That moves the sun in heaven and all the stars.

[1] Three orbs of triple hue. The Trinity.

Next after Dante, the first name of importance in Italian literature is that of Francesca Petrarca, called Petrarch in English. He was the son of a Florentine exile, was born at Aruzzo in 1304, and died at Padua in 1374. He was a scholar and a diplomat, and was entrusted with many public services. Most of his active life he spent at Avignon, at the papal court, or in Vaucluse near by. When he was twenty-three, he met Laura, the beautiful woman with whom he was always after in love, and who was the inspiration of all his lyric poetry. She was the daughter of a citizen of Avignon, and was married, probably to Ugo de Sade of Avignon. She was a good woman whose character was ever above reproach. Petrarch was a very industrious writer. He produced many letters and treatises in Latin, besides a long Latin epic Africa. But his great and deserved fame rests upon his Italian lyric poetry—the Canzoniere. The Canzoniere is divided into three parts: the poems to Laura in life; to Laura in death; and the Triumphs. The Triumphs are inferior in merit to the other two parts. He had studied closely the Provencall poets, and had something of their spirit.

I. To Laura in Life.

SONNET III. HE BLAMES LOVE FOR WOUNDING HIM ON A HOLY DAY (GOOD FRIDAY).

'Twas on the morn' when heaven its blessed ray
In pity to its suffering master veil'd,
First did I, Lady, to your beauty yield,
Of your victorious eyes th' unguarded prey.
Ah! little reck'd I that, on such a day,
Needed against Love's arrows any shield;
And trod' securely trod, the fatal field:
Whence, with the world's, began my heart's dismay.
On every side Love found his victim bare,
And through mine eyes transfix'd my throbbing heart;
Those eyes, which now with constant sorrows flow:
But poor the triumph of his boasted art,
Who thus could pierce a naked youth nor dare
To you in armour mail'd even to display his bow!

— Wrangham.

SONNET XIV. HE COMPARES HIMSELF TO A PILGRIM.

The palmer bent, with locks of silver gray,
Quits the sweet spot where he has pass'd his years,
Quits his poor family, whose anxious fears
Paint the loved father fainting on his way;
And trembling, on his aged limbs slow borne,
In these last days that close his earthly course,
He, in his soul's strong purpose, finds new force,
Though weak with age, though by long travel worn:
Thus reaching Rome, led on by pious love,
He seeks the image of that Saviour Lord
Whom soon he hopes to meet in bliss above:
So, oft in other forms I seek to trace

Some charm, that to my heart may yet afford
A faint resemblance of thy matchless grace.

— Dacre

SONNET XCVIII. LEAVE-TAKING.

There was a touching paleness on her face,
Which chased her smiles, but such sweet union made
Of pensive majesty and heavenly grace,
As if a passing cloud had veil'd her with its shade;
Then knew I how the blessed ones above
Gaze on each other in their perfect bliss,
For never yet was look of mortal love
So pure, so tender, so serene as this.
The softest glance fond woman ever sent
To him she loved, would cold and rayless be
Compared to this, which she divinely bent
Earthward, with angel sympathy, on me,
That seem'd with speechless tenderness to say,
"Who takes from me my faithful friend away?"

-E.(New Monthly Magazine.)

SESTINA VII. HE DESPAIRS OF ESCAPING FROM HIS TORMENTS.

Count the ocean's finny droves;
Count the twinkling host of stars,
Round the night's pale orb that moves;
Count the groves' wing'd choristers;
Count each verdant blade that grows;

Counted then will be my woes.

. . . .

Sad my nights; from morn till eve,
Tenanting the woods, I sigh:
But, ere I shall cease to grieve,
Ocean's vast bed shall be dry,
Suns their light from moons shall gain,
And spring wither on each plain.

    Pensive, weeping, night and day,
From this shore to that I fly,
Changeful as the lunar ray;
And, when evening veils the sky,
Then my tears might swell the floods,
Then my sighs might bow the woods!

    Towns I hate, the shades I love;
For relief to yon green height,
Where the rill resounds, I rove
At the grateful calm of night;
There I wait the day's decline,
For the welcome moon to shine.

    Song, that on the wood-hung stream
In the silent hour wert born,
Witness'd but by Cynthia's beam,
Soon as breaks to-morrow's morn,
Thou shalt seek a glorious plain,

There with Laura to remain!

— Nott.

II. To Laura in Death.

SONNET 1. ON THE ANNOUNCEMENT OF THE DEATH OF LAURA.

    Woe for the 'witching look of that fair face!
The port where ease with dignity combined!
Woe for those accents' that each savage mind
To softness tuned, to noblest thoughts the base!
And the sweet smile, from whence the dart I trace,
Which now leaves death my only hope behind!
Exalted soul, most fit on thrones to 've shined,
But that too late she came this earth to grace!
For you I still must burn, and breathe in you;
For I was ever yours; of you bereft,
Full little now I reck all other care.
With hope and with desire you thrill'd me through,
When last my only joy on earth I left—
But caught by winds each word was lost in air.

— Anon, Ox., 1795.

SONNET XLII. THE SPRING ONLY RENEWS HIS GRIEF.

    The soft west wind, returning, brings again
Its lovely family of herbs and flowers;
Progne's gay notes and Philomela's strain
Vary the dance of springtide's rosy hours;

And joyously o'er every field and plain
Glows the bright smile that greets them from above,
And the warm spirit of reviving love
Breathes in the air and murmurs from the main.
But tears and sorrowing sighs, which gushingly
Pour from the secret chambers of my heart,
Are all that spring returning brings to me;
And in the modest smile, or glance of art,
The song of birds, the bloom of heath and tree,
A desert's rugged tract and savage forms I see.

— Greene.

SONNET LII. HE REVISITS VAUCLUSE.

I feel the well-known breeze, and the sweet hill
Again appears, where rose that beauteous light,
Which, while Heaven willed it, met my eyes, then bright
With gladness, but now dimmed with many an ill.
Vain hopes! weak thoughts! Now, turbid is the rill;
The flowers have drooped; and she hath ta'en her flight
From the cold nest, which once, in proud delight,
Living and dying, I had hoped to fill:
I hoped, in these retreats, and in the blaze
Of her fair eyes, which have consumed my heart,
To taste the sweet reward of troubled days.
Thou, whom I serve, how hard and proud thou art!
Erewhile, thy flame consumed me; now, I mourn
Over the ashes which have ceased to burn.

— Roscoe.

CANZONE III. UNDER VARIOUS ALLEGORIES HE PAINTS THE VIRTUE, BEAUTY, AND UNTIMELY DEATH OF LAURA.

While at my window late I stood alone,
So new and many things there cross'd my sight,
To view them I had almost weary grown.
A dappled mind appear'd upon the right,
In aspect gentle, yet of stately stride,
By two swift greyhounds chased, a black and white,
Who tore in the poor side
Of that fair creature wounds so deep and wide,
That soon they forced her where ravine and rock
The onward passage block: Then triumph'd
Death her matchless beauties o'er,
And left me lonely there her sad fate to deplore.
. . . .
In a fair grove a bright young laurel made—
Surely to Paradise the plant belongs!—
Of sacred boughs a pleasant summer shade,
From whose green depths there issued so sweet songs
Of various birds, and many a rare delight
Of eye and ear, what marvel from the world
They stole my senses quite!
While still I gazed, the heavens grew black around,
The fatal lightning flash'd, and sudden hurl'd,
Uprooted to the ground, That blessied birth.
Alas! for it laid low,
And its dear shade whose like we ne'er again shall know.
. . . .
A lovely and rare bird within the wood,
Whose crest with gold, whose wings with purple gleam'd,
Alone, but proudly soaring, next I view'd,

Of heavenly and immortal birth which seem'd,
Flitting now here, now there, until it stood
Where buried fount and broken laurel lay,
And sadly seeing there
The fallen trunk, the boughs all stripp'd and bare,
The channel dried—for all things to decay
So tend-it turn'd away
As if in angry scorn, and instant fled,
While through me for her loss new love and pity spread.

    At length along the flowery award I saw
So sweet and fair a lady pensive move
That her mere thought inspires a tender awe;
Meek in herself, but haughty against Love,
Flow'd from her waist a robe so fair and fine
Seem'd gold and snow together there to join:
But, ah! each charm above
Was veil'd from sight in an unfriendly cloud:
Stung by a lurking shake, as flowers that pine
Her head she gently bow'd,
And joyful pass'd on high, perchance secure:
Alas I that in the world grief only should endure.

SONNET LXXXV. HE CONFESSES AND REGRETS HIS SINS, AND PRAYS GOD TO SAVE HIM FROM ETERNAL DEATH.

    Love held me one and twenty years enchain'd,
His flame was joy—for hope was in my grief!
For ten more years I wept without relief,

When Laura with my heart, to heaven attain'd.
Now weary grown, my life I had arraign'd
That in its error, check'd (to my belief)
Blest virtue's seeds-now, in my yellow leaf,
I grieve the mispent years, existence stain'd.
Alas! it might have sought a brighter goal,
In flying troublous thoughts, and winning peace;
O Father! I repentant seek thy throne:
Thou, in this temple hast enshrined my soul,
Oh, bless me yet, and grant its safe release!
Unjustified—my sin I humbly own.

— Wollaston.

SONNET XC. THE PLAINTIVE SONG OF A BIRD RECALLS HIS KEENER SORROW.

Poor, solitary bird, that pour'st thy lay,
Or haply mournest the sweet season gone,
As chilly night and winter hurry on,
And daylight fades, and summer flies away!
If, as the cares that swell thy little throat,
Thou knew'st alike the woes that wound my rest.
O, thou wouldst house thee
In this kindred breast,
And mix with mine thy melancholy note!
Yet little know I ours are kindred ills:
She still may live the object of thy song:
Not so for me stern Death or Heaven wills!
But the sad reason, and less grateful hour,
And of past joy and sorrow thoughts that throng,
Prompt my full heart this idle lay to pour.

FROM THE DECAMERON.

The third great name in Italian mediaeval literature is that of Giovanni Boccaccio. He was born in Paris in 1313, and died at Certaldo in 1345. Like Dante and Petrarch he was a scholar and an industrious writer. He wrote some important historical treatises, and many poems, some of which attained some fame. But it is as a writer of prose that he deserves the name he has. In Italy, as in all other lands, there was in the Middle Ages a large body of tales and fables in circulation. In Italy, during the thirteenth and fourteenth centuries, these tales came into literature as Novellas or novels. The Decamerone of Boccaccio is a collection of a hundred such novels or tales. They are derived from many sources, probably not more than three or four of them being invented by Boccaccio. The tale we select is interesting as furnishing the basis for one of Keats' beautiful romantic ballads.

THE POT OF BASIL.

There lived, then at Messina, three young merchants, who were brothers, and left very rich by their father; they had an only sister, a lady of worth and beauty, who was unmarried. Now, they kept a youth, by way of factor, to manage their affairs, called Lorenzo, one of a very agreeable person, who, being often in Isabella's company, and finding himself no way disagreeable to her, confined all his wishes to her only, which in some little time had their full effect. This affair was carried on between them for a considerable time, without the least suspicion; till one night it happened, as she was going to his chamber, that the eldest brother saw her, without her knowing it. This afflicted him greatly; yet, being a prudent man, he made no discovery, but lay considering with himself till morning, what course was best for them to take. He then related to his brothers what he had seen, with regard to their sister and Lorenzo, and, after a long debate, it was resolved to seem to take no notice of it for the present, but to make away with him privately, the first opportunity, that they might remove all cause of reproach both to their sister and themselves. Continuing in this resolution, they behaved with the same freedom and civility to Lorenzo as ever, till at length, under a pretense of going out of the city, upon a party of pleasure, they carried him along with them, and arriving at a lonesome place, fit for their purpose, they slew him, unprepared to make any defence, and buried him there; then, returning to Messina, they gave it out that they had sent him on a journey of business, which was easily believed, because they frequently did so. In some time, she, thinking that he made a long stay, began to inquire earnestly of her brothers concerning him, and this she did so often, that at last one of them said to her, "What have you to do with Lorenzo, that you are continually teasing us about him? If you inquire any more, you shall receive such an answer as you will by no means approve of." This grieved her exceedingly; and, fearing she knew not why, she remained without asking any more questions; yet all the night would she lament and complain of his long stay; and thus she spent her life in a tedious and anxious waiting for his return; till one night it happened, that having wept herself asleep, he appeared to her in a dream, all pale and ghastly, with his clothes rent in pieces; and she thought he spoke to her thus: "My dear Isabel, thou grievest incessantly for my absence, and art continually calling upon me: but know that I can return no more to thee, for the last day that thou sawest me, thy brothers put me to death." And, describing the place where they had buried him, he bid her call no more upon him, nor ever expect to see him again, and disappeared. She, waking, and giving credit to the vision, lamented exceedingly; and, not daring to say anything to her brethren, resolved to go to the place mentioned in the dream, to be convinced of the reality of it. Accordingly, having leave to go a little way into the country, along with a companion of hers, who was acquainted with all her affairs, she went thither, and clearing the ground of the dry leaves with which it was covered, she observed where the earth seemed to be lightest, and dug there. She had not searched far before she came to her lover's body, which she found in no degree wasted; this confirmed her of the truth of her vision, and she was in the utmost concern on that account; but, as that was not a fit place for lamentation, she would willingly have taken the corpse away with her, to have given it a more decent interment; but, finding herself unable to do that, she cut off his head, which she put into a handkerchief, and, covering the trunk again with the mould, she gave it to her maid to carry, and returned home without being perceived. She then shut herself up in her chamber, and lamented over it till it was bathed in her tears, which being done, she put it into a flower pot, having folded it in a fine napkin, and covering it with earth, she planted sweet herbs therein, which she watered with nothing but rose or orange water, or else with her tears; accustoming herself to sit always before it, and devoting her whole heart unto it, as containing her dear Lorenzo. The sweet herbs, what with her continual bathing, and the moisture arising from the putrified head, flourished exceedingly, and sent forth a most agreeable odour. Continuing this manner of life, she was observed by some of the neighbours, and they related her conduct to her brothers, who had before remarked with surprise the decay of her beauty. Accordingly, they reprimanded her for it, and, finding that ineffectual, stole the pot from her. She, perceiving that it was taken away, begged earnestly of them to restore it, which they refusing, she fell sick. The young men wondered much why she should have so great a fancy for it, and were resolved to see what it contained: turning out the earth, therefore, they saw the napkin, and in it the head, not so much consumed, but that, by the curled locks, they knew it to be Lorenzo's, which threw them into the utmost astonishment, and fearing lest it should be known, they buried it privately, and withdrew themselves from thence to Naples. The young lady never ceased weeping, and calling for her pot of flowers, till she died; and thus terminated her unfortunate love. But, in some time afterwards, the thing became public, which gave rise to this song:

> Most cruel and unkind was he,
> That of my flowers deprived me, &c.

Lightning Source UK Ltd.
Milton Keynes UK
UKHW020646040219
336711UK00010B/292/P